KING PEN[G]

Jeremy Reed: Selec[ted]

Jeremy Reed was born in Jersey, Ch[annel Islands. In 1985 he] received the major Eric Gregory Award, and his collection *By the Fisheries* (1984) won the 1985 Somerset Maugham Award. His most recent collection of poetry is *Nero* (1985). He has been described by David Gascoyne as 'the most outstanding poet of his generation'. He divides his time between London and the sea.

Jeremy Reed
Selected Poems

A KING PENGUIN
PUBLISHED BY PENGUIN BOOKS

Penguin Books Ltd, Harmondsworth, Middlesex, England
Viking Penguin Inc., 40 West 23rd Street, New York, New York 10010, U.S.A.
Penguin Books Australia Ltd, Ringwood, Victoria, Australia
Penguin Books Canada Limited, 2801 John Street, Markham, Ontario, Canada L3R 1B4
Penguin Books (N.Z.) Ltd, 182–190 Wairau Road, Auckland 10, New Zealand

By the Fisheries and *Nero* first published by Jonathan Cape Ltd 1984, 1985
After Montale first published in this volume 1987
This selection of poems from *By the Fisheries* and *Nero*,
together with *After Montale*, published in Penguin Books 1987

Made and printed in Great Britain by
Cox & Wyman Ltd, Reading
Typeset in Linotron 202 Plantin by
Rowland Phototypesetting Ltd,
Bury St Edmunds, Suffolk

FOR JAMES LASDUN

Contents

Acknowledgements   11

By the Fisheries [1984]

Composition   15
Buoys   16
Hail on the Rebound   18
Christopher Smart in Madness   20
By the Fisheries   23
Surfers   25
Visiting Hours   27
Housman in Old Age   29
Amen   30
Persephone   31
Elegiacs   33
Death Bed   34
To Him Away   35
An Age Bereft   37
Barn at a Tilt   38
Sea-room   39
Lumber Room   41
Two   42
Dead Hand   43
A Location   45
The Well   47
The Chatter of Magpies   48
Conger   49
Dogfish   51
Mullet   53
Questionably   55
John Clare's Journal   56
Rain   59
Cliff Fires   61
Stick by Stick   63
Tulips   65

Snail   66
Air   67
Filming Couple   69
The Person from Porlock   71
The Storm   73
Giant Surf   75
Pendeen Watch   77
Outgoings   79
Greek Colony   80

Nero [1985]

Spider Fire   85
Wounded Gull   87
Dead Weasels   88
Foxes   90
Rabbits   92
Voles   94
On Fallow Foliage   95
The Middle of Life   96
Goldfish   97
Winter Mullet   99
Bass   101
Worm   103
Burying Beetle   105
Ants   106
Daddylonglegs   108
Drought   109
Blackberrying   110
Red Geraniums   111
Violets   113
Moors   114
Horse Chestnuts   116
Baudelaire's Paris   118
The Irretrievable: Baudelaire   121

8

Baudelaire's Abyss   124
Baudelaire in Middle Age   127
Baudelaire's *Aesthetique*   130
The Treadmill: Baudelaire   133
The Curved Hip: Baudelaire   136
Going Back   139
Kleptomaniac   141
Heirloom   143
Regular   145
Cornering   147
At Midnight   149
The Meaning   150
Bar Stand   152
Smoke on Water   154
The Wake's Departure   156
A Girl in Summer   157
The Deep End   159
Behind the Scene   161
Stamping Ground   162
In and Out   164
Writing a Novel   166
The Music of Blue   168
Pact   170
Apprehension   171
After Horace: Epodes 12   172
Catullus 29   173
After Horace: Epodes 14   174
Nero   175
January   180
Foggy Days   182
Neutral   184
Distribution   185
Momentum   187
Shell Collection   188
Summering   190

Hiving the Light   192
Migration   193
September Cycle   194
Late Year Fog   195
Painting Water   197

After Montale [1985]

Rifts   201
Arsenio   203
Summer   205
The Eel   206
New Stanzas   207
The Customs House   208
At Fiesole   209
Sirocco   210
The Sunflower   211
The Black Trout   212
Point of the Mesco   213
The Shadow of the Magnolia   214
Hitlerian Spring   215
Correspondences   217
Delta   218
On a Letter Unwritten   219
Eclogue   220
Under the Rain   222
Beach in Versilia   223
Times at Bellosguardo   225
Syria   227
Angularity   228
Indian Serenade   229
Wind and Flags   230
Costa San Giorgio   231
Xenia I (1964–6)   232
Xenia II   236

Acknowledgements

The following poems from *By the Fisheries* previously appeared in these publications: 'Buoys' (*Literary Review*); 'By the Fisheries (*Poetry Review*); 'Air' and 'Christopher Smart in Madness' (*Temenos*; 'Air' also appeared in *Waves*); 'Visiting Hours' (*Twofold*); 'Housman in Old Age', 'To Him Away', 'An Age Bereft' and 'Greek Colony' (*Straight Lines*; 'Greek Colony' also appeared in *Aquarius*); 'Conger' (*Glasgow Magazine*); 'A Location' (Gregory Awards anthology); 'Questionably' (Enitharmon Press); 'John Clare's Journal' (Menard Press and *Labrys*); 'Surfers' (*New Statesman*); 'The Person from Porlock' (*London Review of Books*). Six of the poems ('The Storm', 'To Him Away', 'Conger', 'Dogfish', 'Christopher Smart in Madness' and 'Buoys') appeared in the Penguin anthology of new writing, *Firebird 3*.

The following poems from *Nero* previously appeared in these publications: 'Migration' (*Aquarius*); 'Daddylonglegs' (*Field*); 'Heirloom' (*Literary Review*); 'Blackberrying', 'Momentum' and 'September Cycle' (*Poetry Canada Review*); 'Wounded Gull' and 'Rabbits' (*Poetry Review*); 'Dead Weasels' and 'Violets' (*Temenos*); 'The Music of Blue' (*Twofold*); 'Bass' (*Two Plus Two*); 'Cornering' and 'Apprehension' (*Verse*); 'Nero' (*New Directions Anthology* 49); 'Behind the Scene' (*New Yorick*); 'The Deep End' (*Small Schools Anthology*).

By the Fisheries
[1984]

Composition

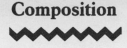

His red silk necktie flares, and moodily
she's turned to watch a tufted duck's apache

black head streak rival the mallard's turban
of iridescent silks, and shelducks scan

the sky's cameo in the lake. The lime
tree smells of rain – a scent come from the shine

of an old pocket in which coins have lain.
The jasmine's musty, and azaleas stain

the water madder rose. It's sharper now
the shower's build-up, and a greylag scows

for shelter. Why it is that two conflict
upon a scale of moods he can't predict

a pattern to's the puzzle, like this lake's
alphabet of V's – web-footed duck wakes

that cut the green silk to a convict's cloth
of arrows. A swan turntables a wreath

on the darkening water, and he draws
his mind back in, edging for words to thaw

a silence, cold as a quartz vein in stone,
and then she's plunging, as her opaline

necklace splits on its string – each green bead's lit
by a raindrop scoring a perfect hit.

Buoys

Punch drunk are worked over,
beleaguered by each sea's
top-spin of swell, lathered
and pitched to queasily

restabilize, they are ochre
pumpkin-heads pocked with rust shale
in a whorl of white water,
grouting like snouts in a pail

in the momentary backwash
of Atlantic welter.
To seagulls they're atolls,
to the tern flying saucers,

and obesely unsinkable,
they are a boxer's nightmare
of a face repeatedly hit
that won't black-out, but stays there.

They are bulk opposing a sea
that never stops running, markers
of dangerous shoals, their bells
warning off intruders

gruffly as farm-dogs. Herded
out across nautical charts,
they are inshore satellites,
playing their rumbustious parts

for all sea-craft. Vigilant bulls
confined to marking time,
they too in their anchorage
tug at a nose-chain,

and snore hoarsely in storm,
the sea waterbug-green,
beneath a sky black
as a cormorant's sheen.

Two I see wintering
at grass in a shipping yard,
veterans of long wars,
their grizzled tonsures hard

with resilience, awaiting
new paint, their cyclopean
eyeballs gone rusty from staring
unlidded at the ocean.

Hail on the Rebound

A fizz, and then the rush is voluble,
hail stones the size of mistletoe berries
are sieved through crevices, clicking marbles

that split, ricochet, and made angular
take off into a frenetic orbit,
lose volume and subside as frosted stars

on asphalt and grebe-crested tufts of grass.
Their cooling meets the temperature of air
that has the surface clarity of glass,

and in the pause between volleys the calm
is urgent with the singing of a thrush
whose notes test the air with the quick alarm

that flattens a cat to liquidity
so that it seems possessed only of eyes.
A single stone falls intermittently –

its rap's the crackle of a robin's beak
tenaciously chipping at a snail-shell,
then the note's faster, and the air vibrates

as though someone was kneading sacks of grain
before they split and poured into a yard.
This time I rush ouside into the lane,

my knuckles stung by the dactylic ring
of dice-sized ice-cubes bouncing back knee-high
from the crown of the road and scuttering

to icy corners. They're like mushrooms grown
up instantaneously before one's eyes.
A sudden gust and each ice-spark is blown

back in my face: I feel my clothes catch light
with the incandescent brilliance of pearls,
and then I'm running and my eyes are bright.

Christopher Smart in Madness

They spare me Bedlam for St Luke's Shoreditch,
who am appointed heir to King David,
and fester here where rabid
cries accompany Battie's enquiry
as to madness, whence comes this divine itch
to see into the limits of the sky?
I trundle God's gold ball in Satan's ditch.

They bait me like a bear. My creditors
are importuning demons who'd usurp
my episcopal claims. They hurt
my fevered head, and festinate the ague,
so that I shrink back in my noisome lair,
and crouch there, distracted, unwitting, vague.
The fire of ADORATION burns my hair.

My wife's a Moabite, a Newbery
for whom I squandered my pen in burlesque
before the angelic lyre struck
my holiness to David. Now I pray
that all hurt things are of one ministry.
Listen, the redbreast sings in February,
appointed angel to our misery.

And I am delivered from London's news,
its pettifogging brawls. Johnson alone
gives meat to a dead skeleton
of words; and came by. How his linen stank,
like mine. His strength prevents him breaking
through to the other side of reason. I drank,
before a red cloud opened in the blue,

and I prayed vociferously to God,
and bound myself to the purgative wheel
which burnt the lining of my soul.

Jubilate Agno, they'd confiscate,
except my mind's like a worm in a clod,
which cut in half can still compose, secrete,
and render consecration to David.

Cuckolded, cheated of inheritance,
I shiver here, and hear the sudden bell
of Staindrop Church. Lilac umbels
chequered the grass, the wild polyanthus,
I picked for one Anne Hope, and then in trance,
saw our heavenly marriage through stained glass.
God's voice was further then. I had distance.

And now a pauper go. My alms are words
of prophecy. God lit my candlestick's
orange and immutable wick,
but still they never see. Harping-irons
prod us to tasks, who cower here in dread,
and see rats catch the bread for which we pine,
and hungry, live upon raw gin instead.

Let Peter rejoice with the white moon fish
that's radiant in the dark, and let attend
Jesus on us, unsound of mind,
who cured Legion. My brethren here despair
of light, and must in other madhouses
repine for day; and go without repair.
I pray so loudly that the others curse.

The prison dampness comes to coat my skin
who venture in God's fire, and see the stone
on the right hand side of his throne
withheld from man. And gold within the dark,
I see the mine of Hell where the napkin
of the escaped Jesus still redly marks
the stone, and brooding on it I see Cain.

21

Outside it rains. I hear a horse collapse,
and men beat it ferociously with sticks.
It died. I pray God for redress
of all animal injuries. Tonight
I wept, and thought to incur a relapse,
and in his knowledge God brightened his light.
Tonight Christ's lantern swings inside this house.

By the Fisheries

The sea's translucent here, slowed to a calm
by an opposing breakwater, a form
of improvised harbour – its concrete arm

projected to oppose a running grey
current that's never still, but turns over
the way a leaf might, caught up in the spray

of a waterfall to expose markings
of jasper and lime as an underside
to galled blues, here contained as in a ring

siphoned off the channel by industry.
Here where a desalination plant churns
its outwash into a let of the sea,

and the zinc buildings of a fisheries
are cantoned above a hollow backdrop,
I stand, fishing that pooled serenity

for mullet, and watch sunlight make a star
on the shards of a broken gin bottle.
The aim's to cast wherever shadows are

composed by cloud, and not the diffusion
of one's image breaking up in water.
I watch my float's spherical orange cone

calligraphize its motion on the glare
that strikes the water like molten lead poured
into a sheet that furnaces on air,

and hangs there in a cobalt flame. A man
trundles an offal barrow to a bin,
and stands a long time with a yellow can,

staring at my immobile silhouette,
pensively tilted back into shadow,
my features guarded by a wide-brimmed hat,

and then deposits what looks like the flash
of a signet ring into the water –
his hollow beer-can lands without a splash.

I don't look up, rather I watch the shoal
jolt with that vibration, and jump like nerves
startling their own reflections back to real.

Surfers

Couched in a recess from the wind I've seen
ravens fly back and forth to this cliff-ledge,
and watched the sea returning, and its sheen

turn bluebottle-blue flecked with indigo,
as though ink dropped into an abalone
accounted for that darkening. The flow

is rapid, and surf blazes across flats
burnished a hard gold by the wind, ribbed sand
planed level as a sheet of glass. In hats

and beach shorts, the surfing crowd congregate
beneath the sea wall, and out of the wind,
absorb the sun's fierce energies, the slate-

like textures of their bodies oiled to bare
both sea and sun. Up here I watch those birds
drop down through a blue crystal of sea air

and comb beached drifts of wrack dried by the heat
to fossil strands where flies fester. Each wave
asserts a resonance – a drumming beat

communicated to the group who tan,
awaiting a heavier lift of surf
to call them to their boards. I watch a man

squat down, his pulse picking up the rhythm
of each new smoking wall of surf that gains
momentum, shot through with light by the sun

to subside with a mulling poker's hiss.
He's like a sentry in his black peaked cap,
maintaining vigil, and at his raised fist

the word is out, and down the beach they race —
these tiny figures running with their boards
into the wind and the blue rim of space.

Visiting Hours

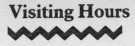

I try to reach you who reverse in years
to a child lost inside a labyrinth,
and it seems you're my son now, not father,
and it is I who must answer questions
by a frightened bedside, and allay fears
that root in you, and by circumvention
of facts, pretend that it's an interval

of rest you're here for, not a terminal
illness; and that this bed, this window pane
dustily framing the roofs of London
is the last corner that you'll come to know
on earth; the ward for four, circumspect walls
of white, the soundless television screen
that's on all day, and the routinal pills

that deaden your cancer's anabasis,
steroids to reduce brain inflammation.
Fifty-eight years without a day's illness,
and now your helplessness is of a child's
fumbling for speech, for a balance that's gone,
and leaves you without co-ordination,
seeking sleep, like a diver gone on down

to find an exit that was always there,
but never used. Each day you go deeper
in that exploration, while we in air
can only call you from a great distance,
and meet you when you surface. Who's farther
from whom? I only know you need me here,
as once you comforted me in nightmare.

You hold my hand as though I were a spool
playing you out lifeline with each visit,
hoping that thread's unbreakable. Your pull

is vibrant at all hours, and the welts cut
each time you awake to panic or fear,
and I can sense your knowledge that you are
a hooked salmon who can't jump from the pool.

The prospect narrows. Standing in the sun,
I see my own death frozen in a beam,
as it will isolate me years later,
and I without offspring. You are my son
in these last weeks. A huge jet lifts over
the city; then the ward reverts to calm.
I too fear the end of visiting hours.

Housman in Old Age

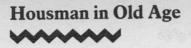

The water's cold not tepid: an austere
face inquisitively feels the razor's
smooth passage induce no sudden bristle
or discomfort. (Once your criterion
for the awesome chill
attendant on a poem's inception.)
A long dormancy's blunted your response,
and if the razor slips, it's clumsiness,
not the sudden impulse of a lyric.
You've mellowed to a specious scholasticism,
and a bachelor's eccentric Cambridge walks.
Such is the age of one who wrote of youth.
The wasted years bay you like a gaunt wolf.

Amen

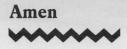

after Georg Trakl

These might be Dürer's hands clasped tight in prayer,
consigned to yellow in an old mirror,
the way sweat cools upon dying fingers
before they freeze. Whoever left these here
was icelocked by the blue of opium,
and left his ghost to brood like Azrael
at twilight over the autumn garden.

Persephone

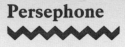

The blue iris streaked with its pheasant's gold –
a sunspot foxing its deep-violet blue,
was what her eye alighted on, the cold
still snowing goose pimples upon her flesh
where she'd bathed in the stream's issue,
a goblet-shaped pool hidden by dwarf pines,
where the crested hoopoe perched on a spine
of rock and sang, and the kingfisher's flash

was like a turquoise shooting-star. Her hands
and feet propelled her with a swimming bird's
motion in water, she who'd had to stand
for hours in front of a mirror to learn
she was of earth, and overheard
the stream's insidious concourse, its bright
current would weave her veins into clear light,
or leave her an illusory heron

composed of water-spray upon a stone.
She'd left her friends paddling, and crossed a glade,
preferring to seek flowers, and hear the drone
of bees alighting on white narcissi;
and didn't see that sudden shade
darken the earth, as though the sun blacked out,
to be answered by an underground shout.
Its echo thunderclapped in the blue sky.

Before her stretched a plain, and asphodels
and the mauve crocus were a coloured rain
entrancing her to stoop, and white umbels
of hemlock caught the breeze. It seemed a jar
had been fitted over the plain,
for not a bird called, and she stood frozen
above the earth in a windless vacuum,
then fear was blinding her with a red star –

31

as a hairline zigzagged to a fissure
beneath her feet; his grasp was like a thorn
that went on growing to a tree, and where
she placed her hands blood ran, and tiny beads
speckled the iris, and the corn
shoots thrusting sunwards. Her head was a cup,
a rapid poured into, breaking it up,
and when the pain subsided, then her need

to know its source was quickened, and she fell
plummeting into a pitch-black spiral,
flight after flight through a vertical well,
his glowering eyes above her, and his knees
pressing her rump into a ball
that twisted in its drop, and when she woke,
her hair was singeing, and she clawed through smoke
to where a dog howled beneath cypress trees,

and found him staring into a mirror
in which nothing showed but a cobalt star
which changed into a man in a tether
hanging upside down. She was turning numb
and felt the pain cool in the scar
he'd opened in her; air shot through her veins,
and she was kiting up above a plain
where men cast crow's shadows, her mouth locked dumb

and leathery before he held the red
fruit of the pomegranate to her lips,
and watched her bite it until her mouth bled,
that sharp sacrament promising rebirth
as a blue shadow of the pit,
but already she knew she would reclaim
her heritage of light, and in spring rain
finger the green shoot thrusting from the earth.

Elegiacs

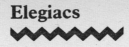

I
A bay so iridescently becalmed
one could have used it as a mirror to
paint a self-portrait. Mullet in haikus
lipped frond: their browsing chimed like bone china
on the water's ultramarine surface.

II
August: we came here the month of gorse fires,
outsiders bronzing naked in the coves,
the sand ribbed like a fishbone. The others
kept to the near shore, burnt bark-brown in oil.
Everything touched crackled with a red flare.

III
Hazed over, mist was the first touch of chill
in a sea garden plumed with pampas grass.
We huddled. The quincunx of a rock pool
was what I thought of, its bright mosaic
an ordered sequence winter tides would cull.

IV
So soon estranged. We stood above the bay,
and watched a flight of martins dip the cape,
and bend into their migrational pull.
We left: two in flight, anxious to escape,
our separation ringing like goats' bells.

Death Bed

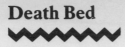

after Po Chü-i
My bed is placed by an unpainted screen,
and sunlight filters through a blue curtain.
Those rapid voices are my grandchildren
inflectionlessly reading me a book,
while I pencil amendments to poems
sent me by friends. Drug-money, and a cook
to heat me wine are my small requisites.
I'll die facing South and facing the light.

To Him Away

Today, our son, my Lord, was much estranged,
   being most lately come
from Gheel, where certain wandering madmen
impressed his youth with black omens,
   so that he walks with tonsured head,
or broods distractedly for hours
   upon the progress of the sun.
I fear he is no longer ours

in sense, and pleasure's to him alien.
   He keeps himself above
a young man's passion to despoil or love,
and is a hawk become a dove.
   I fear the promised union
with Sherbourne's fairest is amiss,
   and increase of estate removes
itself. My Lord, I do distress

you, that I know, you being at the wars,
   and rain making a churn
of every country road. Doubtless we turn
to grief most when there's no return
   by messenger or brumous prayer
I despatch in our cold chapel,
   asking of Christ to move our son
into the light, who strangely fell

into this restless torpor. James, my Lord,
   came speaking with half your
tongue, and half his, as becomes a brother,
and thought to let blood would confer
   upon his nephew quietude.
The need is pressing, for he speaks –
   and this alone gives him pleasure –
of making gold in a retreat,

as lately certain charlatans perform.
   I ask you to renege
all lands promised to him when come of age,
rather, I risk, my Lord, your rage,
   by writing I forbid. Your scorn
at first must not cloud your reason.
   Think, landless, nothing would assuage
your broken pride before the Queen.

The evening bell, and I must late give seal
   to this troublesome news.
I beg you ponder how your son eschews
all reason, before you review
   with what physic we may expel
the mad forebodings of his brain.
   My Lord, as we, pray for our souls.
I send you good tidings: your Jane.

An Age Bereft

∿∿∿∿∿

for Philip Smith

They won't recall our panache, our finesse,
we're outsiders in an age without Proust,
James or Cocteau to notate how style is
a something-not-pronounced, minutiae
of speech, the angle of a handkerchief,
a buttonhole or orchid in a vase,
a mauve ink inscription on a flyleaf;
but more a sensitivity which holds
each mind invulnerable in its privacy,
unencroached on in areas which flinch
a lifetime with the fear of exposure.

                    Rilke, a rose
pressed inside a green vellum book evoked
centuries committed to a girl's diary
by her writing posthumously at a yellow
lacquer desk over which a bee wavered.
A lifetime lived extracting essence like that bee
from moments of evanescent selectivity

is what we look for, the few who remain
divided by a spiderweb from threat
of extinction, recall an autumn night
on an unclouded lawn reading poems,
each knowing it could never be the same
surprised by a red adventitious moon.

Barn at a Tilt

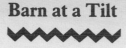

A blue arrow of sky chases across
the brushpoint pebbling of uniform grey;
wet blackberries wear diamond pins of light,
and sparkle like the jet bead of the bay

on which a dinghy cuts a white spadehead
of foam. You've parked your car beside a barn
in which a poet summers with swallows.
A robin taps out a code of alarm

on the tabby markings of a snailshell,
and the rising moon's a sanded mirror
already frosting with its flatfish spots.
We walk towards the headland and defer

speech for reciprocal intimations
of a valediction tightening like wire
around the sinews of a rabbit's paw.
On the heathland someone has lit a fire,

and its subtleties recall gradations
of years cast like pebbles into a well,
so clear that I can see and count them all.
They fidget with the tremor of a bell

the surf rocks. Space becomes our only goal,
walking as though the air was a springboard
projected from the cliff. A bat dipped by,
noiselessly voicing its hunger abroad –

and still without speech we came to the edge,
startled by the blustering of someone,
white-shirted, tieless, the out of season
poet storming his thatched barn at a run.

38

Sea-room

1 Mazarine, and at dusk the holly-blue
   of that frail butterfly pinned on a light
   of dusted persimmon became our view
   at Rock Point, strangers who met in a crag,
   fished by the dipping cormorant and shag,
   both stripped to swim, treading water, upright
   as glass-blue bottlenecks in that gully;
   each stroke formed hemlock clusters on the sea.

2 Your ring, a scarab in mottled turquoise,
   mirrored the sea, your matelot's striped vest
   was scarlet and white, and gold sparks of gorse
   were saffron scallops caught inside your shoes.
   We sat, tented in towels, scoured by the blue,
   both solitary, two blown leaves at rest
   beneath this cliff, where the gannet's poker-
   dive resurfaced with a mackerel's quicksilver.

3 A room in which two leather jackets hung
   upon a nail; a frugal whitewashed shack
   above the breakers, where a bell-buoy swung
   with the tide's rhythm. A cindering heat
   had us dare surfaces with blackened feet,
   running down to the shallows, where a slack
   tide's enervating kitten-ball of sleep
   fluffed up a white swell on the coal-blue deeps.

4 Two strangers, fuelled by a wasp's energy
   to sip at every pollen cup, we grew
   delirious at small things, while the sea
   clouded from manganese-blue to peach-grey,
   and small fishing boats piloted the bay.
   At night on the jetty the lobster's blue
   claws were tied, spidercrabs, shankers, their slow
   grind in a sack was a commando's crawl.

5　This flux and ebb, a sea-change like our moods,
　　mercurial, and drawing back from trust,
　　distempered, like a spider left to brood
　　outside its web, for fear it shatter it.
　　At low tide the rocks were a boiling pit
　　of water dragged out; flies brush-stroked the dust
　　that scalded on the cliff path. In terror
　　we waited for the moon's radiant mirror.

6　A night in which our shadows seemed to grow
　　too huge to control, and the ice-bright stars
　　so visible, it seemed a wind could blow
　　them to embers. Bacchic, crowned with ivy,
　　I thought I saw you by the wildrose sea,
　　blood streaming from your body's frosted scars,
　　and later found you fingering a stone,
　　its bird's-egg speckled clouding – a small moon.

7　They fly into the beam unwittingly,
　　nocturnal shearwaters the lighthouse man
　　throws back into the air for levity
　　so they regain their flight. We too struck blood
　　in a drunken rage, the tide at full flood,
　　your skin so leathered from its scorching tan,
　　I thought you, part man, and part amazon.
　　The dawn's first light was a pink carnation.

8　An empty nail; the seapinks in a jar
　　were all you left, their crowns studded by dew,
　　and I returning found the door ajar,
　　the room so strangely light I knew you gone,
　　the window catching crimson with the dawn
　　then mauvely erupting to cornflower-blue.
　　I sat and counted the seapinks, and heard
　　my blood beat with the outcry of a bird.

Lumber Room

The dark inside smelt of convolvulus
gone musty after rain, and a pappus

of dust thistled each cobweb's tarnished watch-
interior. Light let in by the latch

was a diamond ray tapped out to a code –
a migraine to the spider's eyes to goad

it out of its lilliputian parasol.
Inside, I listened to the martial roll

of small disturbances, and a soot-fall
of air moved with me. It was ritual

this going back upon a scent to find
a burial enacted in the mind –

a child standing before a cracked mirror,
its irezumi mask of bright colours

a solitary Noh drama, while the rain
was a horse's tail swishing flies, a stain

that mouldered in the rafters. Turpentine,
old jaundiced books, tied up trunks, and a wine-

bottle with stalactites of wax were my
discoveries, familiar genies

for a child's magic, listening to his thoughts
name symbols for their colours, while the knot

of the bunched spider stirred like breaking ice
inside the thumb-screw pincers of a vice.

Two

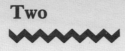

They turn their backs to me; the father's eyes
are crushed blue ice in glass marbles; he flies

his son's kite with one eye into the wind
and one restraining the child who scuffs sand

in a tantrum. Something is very wrong,
the child is disproportionately strong,

his shaved head, concave nose, and dribbling mouth
suggest a mongol. Panting in the drought

of August's sun-kiln, his orange lolly
planted in sand is like a melting tree

that he's abandoned. Crows keep flying back
and forth across the beach, spading at wrack

for what the sea has jettisoned. I watch
the ritual of these two; the shaky match

scratched with one hand the father clumsily
keeps trying to light while observing the sky

with a strained concentration. The child grins
as though his mouth was open on a pin,

his spittle congealing to stalactites;
and now the kite is gusting and its flight

attracts attention. He runs after it,
pursued by a mongrel who jumps to grip

his wrist, and keeps on pulling till it bites.
The father sits back; his cheroot's alight.

42

Dead Hand

His dead hand catches, while the right secures
clothes randomly discarded on a bed,
garments he's seen worn once or twice before,
but kept in store, that velvet suit and red

silk shirt, the water reflections of ties
contrasting lapis lazuli with grey
shot silk – vestiges of a taste that lacked
courage to wear them, now exposed today

on counterpane and floor, a mosaic
to be boxed up and sent to charity
bazaars. His right hand's an inert puppet
that needs constant attention as though he

composed all movement to accommodate
its handicap, nursing it to repose
on safe surfaces. Cautiously he swabs
a thin red line issuing from his nose,

and addresses the empty room, while cold
sunlight whitens the pane, and forms a star
diffusing itself in oblique sunbeams.
He thinks, how in seconds he's come so far

towards the edge of being, that he knows
all time encapsulated in one stare,
and composed of his loss. His dead hand drags,
as on one knee he faces the harsh glare

of sunlight, and tucked beneath his good arm
a bourbon bottle's cradled. Down below,
the reverberation of stalled traffic
makes him conscious of the open window,

43

he slumps by, quickened by the frosted air,
and looks across at a removal van,
and concentrates on its blanketed wares,
his dead hand gummed to an open paint can.

A Location

It seemed part of an aerial photograph,
hatched in with blue and red tessellations,
and somewhere central, a black reservoir,
or place it the other way round, the hole
is in the sky, but not facing the earth,
and those hatchings are perhaps jet vapour
building in space a defence location

or fuelling-rig. Both are conjectural,
and Dwight, who flew a private monoplane,
surveyed the coast around, marshland and shore,
but found nothing improbable, no bore-
hole, nor Ministry of Defence sky-well –
aircraft had been known to clean disappear
before our eyes, then years later return,

pilotless, nosing down upon the dunes,
their body metal eroded by rust,
but of that time-fissure, we had no clue,
and thought of it as extra-sensory,
some pick up on the pilot's brain rhythm,
wrenching the aircraft up, but how it flew
was the enigma, for all lives were lost,

and no astrophysicist determined
correlatives between our coast and sky-
ceiling. Each day we'd hear Dwight's plane survey
our coastal purlieus, and patrol the bay,
looking for something we had come to dread
as right beneath our feet, but to our eyes,
invisible. We'd used telepathy

as a means to communicate secrets,
for centuries, and sometimes the flashback,
or failed intersection, would in seconds

45

so alter a man in body and mind,
we didn't know him, and this constant threat
was always with us, and in the beyond,
that so preoccupied us with its black-

holes, and temporal traps. We tried again
to find an ordnance survey that might show
parallels with the photograph we'd found
in a crashed aircraft; the panel surrounds
were still lit up, as though no lapse of time
had occurred, before its hitting the ground
without a pilot, and devoid of fuel.

And when Dwight disappeared that afternoon,
it came as no surprise, the midge-like drone
of his engine, suddenly extinguished
in the clear blue. We wished him quickly dead,
and knew we'd find the aircraft on a dune,
a week or month or year from now with red
and blue clouds round an upside-down black sun.

The Well

A concentrated bore-hole for the sky
this one has centuries of still brooding,

and a sharp kleptomaniacal eye
that tricks your features from you like a ring,

and reduces them to a cameo
a lilliputian shrinking. Afloat,

I'm poker-faced, and subject to the sky's
caprices, blurred like a face flaring up

behind a windshield in a blinding star
of sunlight. Peeka-boo Peeka-boo chimes

the head I am in its leaning over
inquisitively, and the rim is bean-

grey, chilled with perennial cold-storage,
no drought has ever consumed at its source.

If there's a bottom clouded with vintage
leaf-mould, mouthfuls of the wind's deposit,

its opacity would tarnish a rod,
but is otherwise settled in its bed.

I stay transfixed, the well's concavity
is textured like an unripe blackberry,

the walls tapering to an umbrella
that's rolled, and round it skirt drowsy horse-flies.

I rise, a man with distended knuckles
retrieving from ten feet a monocle.

47

The Chatter of Magpies

Querulous, hackingly raw; their chatter's
repetitious, ascending a scale
of rapid gutturals –
a football rattle devolving slowly
or a zinc bowl clattered by hail.

I listen at the wood's edge. Windy elms
lodge a voice gone with anglo-saxon-
heckling an old adage,
and now two gust up, dropping to hedges,
planing to stand tail-up on a stone,
or flick the liquid eye of a cow-bath,
nervous, as soon gone

to a footfall, one high to an oak-stub,
the other low down, luminous in the wind,
their incantation unriddling
the beetle's path, the snailshell's drum.

Conger

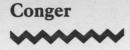

A conger's world is tubular, it means
seeing things thinly through a gun-barrel
from the point of view of the bullet-head
that's primed to fire, the fist-sized, clam-tight jaws

more deadly in their lock than a bulldog's.
They'll shave a finger off with precision,
clean as a horse bite, or close round a hand
and leave it as taut gristle strung on bone.

The colour of beached wrack, or an old tom
that's greying, these inhabit wrecks, or lairs
from which their protruding head is streamlined
like a grounded jet's. Fastened to a spar

they'll fight on a short fuse, and savagely
bite free of suction pads, working to grip
the powerful torsion of the body's girth.
In biting, their mouth opens from a slit

to an alsatian's wide full-toothed gullet.
Conger stay low, anchored to the sea-bed,
solitary killers holed up in their dens,
they mostly go unchallenged, like this head

which would swallow a sewer-rat or cat
washed out to sea; engorge it, and lie low
until nightfall, and then seek out new prey,
killing with a psychopath's will to slow

the moment to all time. Dragged to the air,
a conger barks, and if not killed outright
will live a day, and still retaliate.
This black boothead dazzled by a boat-light,

come loose of the hook, might jump at a throat,
and drag a man down, who stands shrinking back,
petrified at this one to one combat;
a jerky lighthouse twitching through the black.

Dogfish

A sensibility of teeth; down there,
plumb-bottom, where the light is diffused smoke,
and what moves dares that green opacity,
is where one finds you, your round toe-capped snout

raised at the height of a rat-trap from sand
shelving to stone where the conger's snake-head
stokes in its rock lair, and decapitates
an unsuspecting wrasse. What are the dead

to the sea's predators – the millions
of carrion subsumed daily, eaten
before they're dead, or falling to the depths,
scavenged? Nothing has time to go rotten

or stiffen out. The sea would eat the sea
if it had jaws, not the mere force of weight.
And this one, lacking a shark's toothed bonnet,
is still ferocious, and its gut a freight

of green crabs, wrasse, and the sand-stippled plaice.
Spotted, its desert-tank markings disguise
its basking, dredging the sea-floor at night
for flesh split open, fig-ripe, mauve. Its eyes

are set at a pig's angle to its snout,
a lesser shark, it is lobotomized
of the insatiable rip-cord to kill.
The one I hooked had never realized

that space is everywhere there isn't sea,
lashing out on the boat-boards, blinded by
a hurricane lamp, spotted like a log
coming to life, agonized with surprise

at a split-second world that's alien.
For man the reverse process would punch out
his oxygen, and cramped into the cold,
he too might cry, and pressure freeze his shout.

Mullet

A feather fall's a meteorite's crater
to these, so sensitive to sound, water

they pass through seems to chime; a leaf's tremor
will send them like a bird into cover

because a shadow's a predatory
antenna of the human eerily

preceding a foot's performing echo.
The light flares citron in the warm shallows

where mullet browse in a blue calm or bolt
out of the water – an exploding cork

exchanging elements in a rainbow
of vaporizing spray. Sometimes their slow

inquisitive brooding is like a cat's
translating everything to smell, their slate

bodies warily somnolent or gone
like shooting-stars should a shadow become

a superimposition on their sky –
a staining in of features that won't dye

the sunstruck surface of the world they seem
about to break through after lipping green

weed round a jetty or patting a bread-
crust clockwise round a circle. How they feed's

with the same delicacy as they play
with an angler's bait nosing it away

in pendulum fashion. A quicksilver
flash of a belly and the shoal shivers

like a glass breaking – and in bright splinters
converge as an arrowhead streaking where

the water's deeper, and with blunt lips scroll
the surface into liquid parasols.

Questionably

Questionably hexagonal, certainly mauve,
and not forgetting Officer, for courtesy,
is how I described the lenses and frames
of the getaway driver, how he'd left
                              rutted tyre-treads
in braking quickly, turning full-circle,
mounting the pavement for a hit and run.
It happened with that indivisible rift
between lift-off and the airstrip's contact,
                              you know that shift
that's not spatio-temporal, it's like
finding a mirror is not glass but sky
                              one's sucked into
and out of as phenomena that haunt.
We don't want metaphors but incident
came the reply, as I jacked a lighter
                              and remembered
one doesn't when talking direct to the police
interpolate speech with meditative
                              smoke. He did.
I would have enumerated but he
had lost the colour of his eyes, while two
green sequins sparkled on the black leather
                              of my passenger-
seat. I saw his mind figuring out how
to retrieve them without asking. Stretcher-
bearers hurried a red blanket over
                              the victim
and departed, and with them too, the crowd.
I knew a warrant to search my car would
be his logical tactic, but instead
                              he placed dark glasses
on, quavered, then shot himself through the head.
I had to resume interrogation.

John Clare's Journal

Conjunctivital, lame, his nose dripping,
I teach a poor boy and refuse his coin,
and would rather have him read Thomson's Spring
than pore over figures scrawled on a slate.
Outside it rains, and my chrysanthemums,
claret, canary-yellow, white, agate,
show double flowers; and it rains
over Helpstone, and mires the country lanes.

For months, uncommonly depressed, I've sat
and watched the seasons fail, and felt a dark
oppress me, and I've stared out like a rat
from a wood-pile, terrified when I die
my sins will twist like ivy round a bark,
and leave me a lost wraith. Sometimes I cry,
and fear my family's ruin.
Everywhere the red crackle of autumn

lights brief fires; crimson hip, haw, glossy sloe,
hawthorn, and plum-black bryony berry
are winter portents, and my asters glow
in their pied embers. The same pious books
arrive from Radstock, and Taylor defers
my proofs away in London town. A rook
fares better on sparse carrion,
than I the proceeds of my rusty pen.

And still they linger, Billing's late swallows
fan the burgundy air of October
and with their late departure, I'd follow
into the blue sky, and be free. My themes
are no more fashionable than Bloomfield's were,
and he too, starved. Twice I've risen from dreams,
imagining my children laid
out as corpses by a potato spade.

And now that seasonal star, the Michaelmas
daisy, shows in blue clusters, and yellow
ruffles of chestnut leaves stipple the grass.
The little harvestbell quakes in the wind,
ragwort and marjoram linger below
the hedgerows, and twist thin threads, like my mind,
that's racked and vague. Sometimes I see
my own double madly pursuing me,

and then I cower for days in a wood,
or take to the road with gypsies, broken,
and better drunk. A poet's understood
a century too late; men badger words
into affected grace, an unspoken
eloquence, with grammar a two-edged sword,
soon rusty, cast into a pool
where books are ballast for the ship of fools.

Twelve months to set a title page; small fame
for I who charm a lyric from the air,
and suffer quibbling editors who blame
me for my wrong spelling. In Lolham Lane
I found dwarf polopody, and read Blair,
and listened to the slow, fly-flashing rain
tinkle in the flood pits. Alone,
my mind becomes one with the grass and stone.

Better to be a botanist, and mark
each seasonal change, and what's peculiar
to one's native region. A huge crow carks
above me, and for three minutes I've timed
a snail's progress over a slender spar
of twig. Thirteen inches: a track aligned
without a shift to left to right:
such close-up conditions a poet's sight.

A coppled crowned crane shot at Billing's pond,
a gypsy wedding over at Milton,
or a rare white maidenhair fern or frond
distracts me from the melancholy hours
I sit and ponder over Chatterton,
or muse upon the coloured plates of flowers
in Maddox's Directory;
the white peony and red anemone.

They say Byron uses a whip upon
whatever woman inspires him to verse,
and then hangs her up as a skeleton
for crows to peck. Humbled on a cart track,
my inspiration's more a wolf-eyed curse
that keeps me penniless, nosing the black
tunnels a mole snouts in my brain,
vacant for hours, and hatless in the rain.

I dreamt I died last night, or else I fled
into an unfamiliar country,
enclosure had parcelled off, and instead
of finding refuge, I was hunted out,
and forced to stare into a bear's red eyes
and dance with it on a rail-line. A shout
started me, and a bailiff's grip
on my shoulder, worked up and split my lip.

I sit, tussled as my limp hollyhocks,
and watch a beggar pass. Driven from farms,
men scavenge aimlessly; the gypsies knock
and fiddle me a tune. Today I fear
a black shape that has spindle legs and arms,
and grows to envelop the sodden shire.
I am a wart between its eyes,
and yet I blow a grassblade while I cry.

Rain

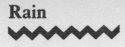

Suddenly I'm astigmatic,
the horizon's a fine paint brush,
each hair's width bristle multiplied
to a pinstripe commuter crush,

that slants diagonally as wind
shifts verticals to map hatchings,
then straightens back to curtain rods,
or needle lines in an etching:

we count each drop's munificence.
Rain multiplies like pennywort,
thumb-tacks of blood on a dry road
darkening to an oilskin, each rut's

an eye-bath for the sky to see
itself in a jigsaw pattern
all over a county, surprised
at angular-sharp reflections,

and how the earth's a mirror turned
over to expose a dull back,
unlike the sea reflecting each
nuance of the sky track.

And in its sound resembles sand
filtered into a human ear,
or torrentially voluble,
water slapping a dark pier;

each bead is like a pheasant's eye,
a rainbow skeined on a globule,
a moon-model to the quick ant.
The yellow pear beside the wall's

59

a lifeboat man lit up by spray.
The rain subsides; drip-drop drip-drop
a form of Chinese torture –
each flower's running on the spot.

Cliff Fires

By day the road's a sheet of hammered tin,
a quicksilver spine snaking into hills
above the cliff, and in the distance thin

curlicues of haze are chalk-dust powdered
on cerulean, and ignite at noon.
Crouched in the shade I'd watch nervous lizards

pulse in the heat, then bolt like forked lightning
into a maze of stones. Each tip of grass
crackled with current, and the kestrel's wing

cast a shadow so still it seemed composed
of the landscape, and not a fierce trip-wire
to bring that bird down vertically, its red

eyes bloody like sirloin. Always the reek
of char was imminent, a dusting blaze
that would cinder a heath, and then a week

later, strike with its circling fire elsewhere –
leaving as residue black rings of ash.
For hours I'd sit here squinting at the glare

as though I stared into a bright mirror
in which I didn't show. Sometimes a gull
would cry out in air that was a razor

polished to hairfine-blue. And when he came,
that strange boy on an afternoon when heat
made coals of pebbles, and the bee hung flame

on the gorse flower, I knew no surprise
at his arrival here, his shuffling gait,
dowsing the furze with petrol on the rise

above the bay, while overhead the sky
furnaced to white heat, and the kestrel dropped,
kicking up dust round the vole's tiny cry.

Stick by Stick

A stoked temper's a big cat in the blood,
and flickers of heat lightning tell me that
the imminence of your unleashed outrage
will suddenly strike like a ball a bat

sends crashing to the boundary. All day
the air's been touchy as a nettle patch,
and breathing in the sultry heat I smell
the crackle of a gorse fire a flipped match

sets blazing in crisp furze. If there's a leak
it taps like an oil drip on a wet road,
a blood-count spiralling to combustion,
so that the red fleck in your eyes explodes

to the wild bloodshot of an outpaced horse.
The room contracts, and its rice-paper walls
threaten to let the neighbours in; I hear
your fist beat a hornet's nest to a squall,

each irascible word, armed with a sting
that goes so deep, I come to doubt that we
are human in this combat, locking skulls,
squid-eyed, reduced to a monstrosity

we doubt as real, but think we act the parts
in a blood-letting; a wolf spider's itch
to entice the male to white sexual heat,
then pick its eyes out in a bone-dry ditch

before the rain storm floats both on the froth
of its torrential stream. We gag for air,
clumsy as seals, wading in divers' boots,
cumbersome, frazzled by the lightning's glare,

63

two wasps simmering over shattered jars
of jam, a broken chair, smashed tabletop,
licking our sores amongst that jellied flow,
too tired to go on, and too mad to stop.

Tulips

These have the reticence of pedigree
breeding, an overstrained, suave dignity

that keeps a poker-grip on things; a tight
refusal to open out to the light,

adamant, in their baronial excess
of colour, torch-bearers under duress

to hold their cool composure for three weeks
in strains of scarlet, mauve, crimson with streaks

of gold, flaming tangerine and dove-white.
Their haughtiness is nerves; each scion's fright

is premature collapse, the palsied shake
that starts a tulip's death; the centre breaks

to reveal a shell crater; each petal
resisting a quick coronary fall,

leaves six blackened candle-wicks as stamen –
a burnt out candelabra on a stem . . .

Tagged with insignias, Abbu Hassan,
Cape Cod, Dragon Light, they resist the rain,

immaculate, close-ranked, a furnace glare
of colour maintained with their special flare

to avoid thought of their future decline,
goblets revealing on both sides the wine

of their rich fermentation, while the bee's
their gold-striped headdress and emissary.

Snail

Is about strategical encampments;
    and is a cosmos to itself
with one inert survivor, not intent

on exploration, but lives snail-aeons
      in contraction, its antennae
closed down, its instinct to become a stone,

its tattersalled markings those of a grey
      tabby, and in its camouflage
inscrutable, is squat, sedentary,

odd like a parked invalid's bubble-car,
      and is laired up behind the dislodged
stone in a hole in the wall. Held askew

it's marzipan-green, or if picked hollow,
      the simple involution of
an ear's its likeness; grit rattles in there.

What are a snail's dimensions? The rotund
      completion of a smooth pebble,
all angularity erased: its mind

not even coming on in wet weather
      when its track is of white trefoil –
an oil freighter's slow passage of silver,

but antennae raised, a jelly-baby
      commando weighted down, but sure
of its passage, moving deliberately

to some inexplicable horizon,
      over a flatland bushed by moss;
its snipers taking refuge from the rain.

Air

Rain water brushed from a swift's pointed wings
on to an eyelash or a spider's web
is how I like to think of the exchange

of altitudes, a vibrant resonance
on this gusty day with birds ticking South
through a needle's eye, each propelled in trance

to dare luminous wind-shafts, and one feels
the elasticity of their wing-pull
in the air's simmer – the twitch of their pole

asserting gravity. The earth transfers
their arrowed passing as the aftermath
of hooves. I crouch down low and consider

the one vertical between me and space
that's flying westwards with the Atlantic,
and watch a singular whitewashed lighthouse

bulb on its rock. Out here the pulse of air
tingles with light hexagonals, I see
it transformed into design and colour

such as the intricacies a snowflake
contrives in fashioning its slow descent.
I sense those sharp intangible facets

pass through me, diamonding the light the way
hail flashes on a heated shovel's back,
or a cormorant's sheen glistens with spray

that smokes on its alighting. Sea and sky
in one illimitable rush of blue
open up light worlds, and the tern's shrill cry

67

untranslatable holds me static here,
given over to such fluidity
I am become a component of air.

Filming Couple

They've stayed on late; he writes, his guernsey sleeves
are holed; and in the land a shrew reddens
with the hawberries and galled alder leaves –

it might have been her car, back from filming,
she's conspicuous here with slashed dresses,
and careless of curtains when undressing

might be a cynosure for a voyeur
cat-flattened in bracken. One knows these things,
there's something wrong, the gin-empties are clear,

so too their emotions darkening like sloes
to distil an intemperate spirit.
She's made up for the Rose and Crown, and shows

a copiousness of flashy, fishnet leg,
but keeps a cool hauteur. He seldom calls.
He works at night or walks their collie dog

across the heath. They seem prepared to stay,
despite the summer's end, and back in town
their unanswered telephone's less each day

a hotline to openings, to filming news.
Here they're cut off, and if frustration grows
their rows are silent, or else kept so low

a window might vibrate without a voice.
Passing their garden I saw deaf-mute signs
become fingers leaving marks on a neck.

And then the grey one came, the director,
or so we learnt, and in pink cotton jeans
escorted her to the pub, his fingers

resting in conversation on her knee,
and unreservedly climbing higher,
and free of pocket bought generously

a last round of doubles for the locals.
Then she was gone; we glimpsed her last of leg
flash in her car, and watched the elm leaves fall

into its parking space. The men stayed on,
one writing filmscript, the other always
about to leave, but busy with a film.

The Person from Porlock

At first, there was no cause for suspicion,
the gentleman rooted in solitude,
had taken possession of a small farm,
and rarely showed. We'd seen him walk the lane,
encumbered by a trunk on arrival,
a scholar, so we heard, and indisposed,
given over to verse and reverie:
attentive about his despatch of mail,
perhaps distracted, but not sinister.

Then one night, woken by the discomfort
of a nagging tooth swabbed in laudanum,
I noticed that his light still burned; the shriek
of an owl scruffing a vole in the brake,
made me shiver at this man's blue candle
and protracted lucubrations. Women
on swearing fealty to the devil
had been turned into hares: confecting charms
was still a distillation of our parish

superstition. My wife wore a toadstone
to ward off ills that bedevil the noon,
and creep sinuously down the gnarled lane
in the shape of a black cat, or magpie.
I raked the whitened embers of the fire,
and huddled there, despite the summer air's
chartreuse and apple-green. A yellow moth
beat at the pane; and dawn was in the sky,
when she I'd left came down, and found me there;

but I disclosed nothing. Later that day,
I saw him scrutinizing the hedgerows,
where blue speedwell and the wild raspberry,
red dead-nettle, and the mauve dwarf-mallow
could be found by the contemplative eye.

His pallor scared me, and he seemed to look
backwards into his head, as though the sky
had made a compact circuit in his skull.
I hailed him, but he never once looked round,

only walked on in abstraction, and seemed
to utter words as an incantation,
and then retraced resolute steps back home,
and didn't show again that day. I sat
down on a stone and watched a goldfinch preen
the blazing pansy colours of its breast,
and found myself without the laudanum
to dull the viper in my tooth, so thought
to call upon that wayward, racked, person,

and ask the use of a strong anodyne.
I sat for hours in cold trepidation,
fearing to knock, and he, as though possessed,
scratched lines across a page, and when the pain
was greater than my own superstition,
I rapped loudly. He still appeared to dream,
and looked unseeingly right through my head,
as though the page was on the other side.
I said, there's something wrong, and grabbed his arm.

The Storm

A wasp's vibration in a gorse-flower,
that orange flame belling the wings' motion,
was how it seemed miles distant, the tremor

of a needlehead dropped from a great height
into the uncorked bottleneck we cooled
in a sea-pool. All afternoon the light

blazed iridescently ultramarine
on a sea surface fixed like an eye-glass
into the peacock of the horizon;

the hours afloat, and a torpid sea-bell,
leisurely tinkling; and you with a pen
and red ink, fashioned a memorial

to the dead seagull found upon the cliff
in our descent. A gruff buzz of black flies
sounded like a kitten's purr on the path

as they stippled that carrion. And down
below, the calm was eerie, and the lull
seemed like the sky and sea stood still, one calm

reflection, lacquered over with gold flecks
in lapis lazuli. We trod water,
or lay immobilely upon our backs

cushioned by the salt bay; and then it grew
this hairline of cobalt, to a fissure
of massing cloud, an ink-dot in the blue

expanding to a welled concentration
of angry mauves, and marbled quartz, and red,
and we could hear the thunder's vibration

73

stalk like a big cat growing voluble
behind the incandescence of its cage.
Then rain, each drop shiningly audible,

clopping into the sea, and shimmering
with a dragonfly's bright translucency,
each globule expanding to a white ring.

We took refuge before the downpour steamed
cleansingly through crevice and flaw, and smoked
skywards. You drew the lightning flares as red

unskewered spiral hairpins jumpingly
illuminating a cobalt skydrop,
while I saw the future, a butterfly

escaping its chrysalis, and on stone,
resting a while, before the longer flight,
sure like the migrant swallow of its home.

Giant Surf

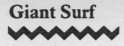

for Michael Armstrong

We can't locate its place of origin,
this running wall, and its each successor
that breaks a mile out on a reef, then runs

at the gradient of a razor blade,
slightly atilt, and is the pilot wave
of that fomenting wreath of swell that's stayed

by opposition of a barrier,
and gaining momentum flicks the white crest
it inclines vertically, then waterfalls

into the wave's advance, and white water
boils dazzlingly at three times a man's height,
and expends itself in measured thunder

across the wide flat of Atlantic beach,
and in its outgoing rebuffs, but can't
impede, the next wave's towering overreach

that scuttles surfers, who in red and blue
attempt to choreographize each new
breaker's overhang, then fallen, review

the bay's slate-blue corrugations for that
one freak wave climbing to obliterate
the skyline, and on whose crest they'll lie flat,

pinpointing balance, vibrant in the light
of the spray's iridescence, until thrown,
they are towed forward, and surface to fight

the backlash that will wash them out to sea,
and winded, bask awhile in the shallows,
bodies aglow with that salt energy,

as though light formed a film on their torsos,
and left their flesh-tones a beaten silver.
They stand there, twenty of them, flecked with snow,

wading back into breakers, slipping free
into their element, while the sheer air
rings with each new wave's volubility.

Pendeen Watch

The kestrel's polestar in blue air
magnifies a pooled radius,
a death-trap lens to whatever
flickers across that treacherous
target-spot filtered to a ring
of blazing gold – the least quiver
brings that bird down upon a string.

On the horizon a white flaw
luminous as a mill-pond
reddens like a flame-tipped straw
the wind fans into embers round
a tanker's dead-squat biscuit tin,
and in that peacock's eye the squall
gravitates to a diamond pin.

And here where the Atlantic's bean-
green's turbulent with pitched groundswell,
I watch a rockpool's mallard sheen
cloud over like a darkened well
gulls drop into, and breakers grind
the cliff's underpinning, bracken
uncoils to goldleaf in the wind.

In a flash the bay's a mirror
reversed to show its blackened side,
blue mackerelings, and dulled silver
steam to a grey rain, and the tide's
mist with a voice. The foghorn wails
from the lighthouse, and a tanker
runs down the channel with the gale.

Around the coast from the Brisons
to Three Stone Oar, farm lights are on,
orange stars in granite hewn stone

eclipsed as the dead monotone
of the foghorn's cowsick bellow
goes out into the sky's frogskin . . .
Waves crash into the caves below.

And later the powerful white beam
of Pendeen Watch will nervously
punctuate the fog with sixteen
flashes a minute, eerily
shot through its quartz crystal prism
that revolves upon mercury.
The light transmits with a white hum.

I make my way back on a road
bubbling with rain, not a car-light
can wash through fog, squat as a toad,
in the warp of the Cornish night,
and shelter in a ruined barn,
as round the coast a flare explodes
and that red signal means alarm.

Outgoings

I
Immemorial the tern's cry
and the rain beading the haw
and the scarlet crab-apple,
eye-pupil bright crystals
on fuchsia, despoiled now
lilac and verbena, all
held in a globe of memory
poised to break like a rain star.

II
No finger-ring could hold
us, not sapphire or turquoise
on a thin band of gold
anchor the pulse. Rather
I'd be alone on jagged outcrop
facing the white Atlantic blaze
of surf hammered quicksilver,
askance like the petrel
daring the storm wave.

III
Sea-kale and sea-campion
their saline hardiness
sempiternally endure.
With us, a valediction
beneath a transient rainbow,
here today and gone
forever like swallows
unable to find a home.

Greek Colony

A sea the green of a butterfly's wing
idles to mid-ebb, and lazily oils
rather than runs. On dark reefs surrounding

the bay, men sunbathe in a mellow heat
that's gone by four o'clock in September.
Already small hotels are boarded up

preliminary to impending gales.
And if you don't come here, where do you go,
I hear the older say; they know the law

about establishing greek colonies,
and are more frightened how the winter long
they must live on the summer's memories.

Already they've thinned out like cormorants
when waters yield bad fishing. Some in twos
fidget, but aren't in pairs; the ugly can't.

I walk out, sanded by the season's dust,
and see the round blue metal beach-table
that crowned our rock, removed for fear of rust

erosion with the huge September tides.
Everything's disbanded or disbanding:
the season bodes departures, suicides.

Summer's like a roman candle, but brief;
the tan acquired, the grottoes sunbathed in
turn desultory like the red-edged leaf.

I watch a man dive off the furthest point,
and bask nakedly in the tepid calm:
the rock for warning's tipped with yellow paint.

And that reef's terminal. Beyond, current
insidiously joins the rip-tide's race,
and coastal beacons plangently descant.

We pour chilled wine into beakers and drink,
facing the horizon, the dunlins' shrill,
and beyond that, each his own personal brink

of fear and loneliness. Already waves
are heightening with the incoming tide,
and each still adamantly disbelieves

the end of summer, holds to the late sun,
like birds in migration, half turning back,
unsure it's not lonelier to go on.

Nero
[1985]

Spider Fire

The popping crackle of dry sticks, the hiss
of catching gorse and broom, had routed out
all small things from the undergrowth, fieldmouse
and shrew, the glinting tick of the grass-snake,
squirrel and weasel, touchpaper-rabbits,
the conflagration spreading, red and blue
quiverings of flame quick to overtake
the fire's orange centre, timothy grass
and thistle sucked into the twitching crack
of the irregularly sheeting wave,
birds had gone in advance of the smoke plume,
rooks heckling in their flapping sky traffic,
chased off by a shuffling necklace of stones,
marigold, scarlet, crazy yellow whirrs
jumping a cow-gate, scorching the farm track . . .

What was the fire's shock through a spider's eyes?
The agelena's horizontal web,
pegged to a blackthorn hedge, scintillating
with rainbow filaments, male and female
telephonic in their alarm signals,
the vibrant nerves unleashed from a tight ball,
acrobats dropped down to the maze-forest
of verticals, a field away the roar
gaining in volume, everywhere a migratory
diaspora of insects, tunnelling,
feeling forward with bristling antennae,
the tenacious marauding wolf-spider
running across hairline fissures, halting
like someone pulled up short by a mirror;
some missing legs, armour-plate or an eye,
embattled hunters chased out of the field
by a seismic explosion, shivering
in the long drag of smoke, their collective
panic inducing a telepathy,
a radar bleep signalling the way out.

85

I watched from the hill's summit; a black hoop
ironed into the shire was a ring of ash
incinerating insects in its char.
The farm was black struts, ember-glowing spars.
Some must have made it to the other side,
two spiders having crossed a continent,
digging in, letting the earth still, aware
they'd made it, smoke-blind, too tired to hide.

Wounded Gull

Wind shifts the earth's face: grit and topsoil run
ticking through crevices, a migration
of tiny particles hissing inland;
wind blinds the red eyes of rabbits with sand,
gulls huddle inshore snowing down on farms,
already the Atlantic's beached a score,
a poulterer's accident, vertebrae
and necks smashed, plump bodies fouled by oil,
they're sucked back and thrown out by each wave's roar,
its dynamited blasting across flats.
What the sea ejects is misshapen, flogged
into the bare components of itself,
slatted, forcibly pitched into debris,
roiled back and forth, scoured pristine by the salt.
I came across dunes, intermittently
dropping into a hollow for shelter,
the wind pressing my brain back to a charge
that flickered like a light in a tunnel,
a fish forcing the opposing current,
and came down to the beach; flooding runnels
kept draining into the torrential surf.
I stood as a bird does facing the wind,
my toe stubbing the petrified shiver
of a gull dislodged from its bone structure,
the collapsed wings trailing, the bloody skull
showing the underside of its fracture.
I could have kneaded it into a ball,
and lobbed it back into the sea's mouth,
its twitching seconds of life dependent
on what few nerves still remained unsevered.
I took it back with me to the seawall,
and buried it, that too no permanent
act of consignment, but something the wave
or wind would upturn, and shake from its bones.
Tomorrow the flood tide would find its grave.

Dead Weasels

I found them hanging, strung up on grey cord,
five of them, gagged together with jackdaws,
the branch weighted like a poulterer's hook
with carrion worn through to their skeletons,
the walnut-sized ivory skull of a rook
had come loose of its rain-moulded bark-stiff
feathers, flushed on dead leaves no fox would sniff.
Dead silence, the wood stark, old beech, old elms,
defiantly rooted against the cold,
and, at the field's edge, rabbit diggings, flint
thrown up on the furrow. The light was gold
on plum-stained brambles. Somewhere else a gun
was barking sporadically at pheasants.
I swung the weasels round to catch the sun,
their long, slender bodies hung vertical,
the fur a straggling ripple on the bone
was like a current chased out in a stream,
the forepaws stylized, were two brittle hands
raised in supplication. The vice-locked head
seemed more a conger's raised to fight the gaff,
the jaws open upon their needle teeth
as though frozen in the bloody second
of ripping into a mole or chicken,
fast night-hunters who companion the owl's
plummet at a leaf-tick. These had their skulls
protruding through an envelope of fur,
crisp to a dryness that the thumb could peel,
rain-beaten fossils gone to matted rope
stringily twined, they looked like effigies
of a demonic rite without the pins.
I cut two down and placed them in a sack,
victims who'd raked the copse for pheasants' eggs,
and sucked them dry. They still had fine whiskers,
minute spiders bunched in the eye sockets.
Their combined weight was less than a finger,

their volatility still composite
in their death agony. Rooks and ravens
were thronging back in droves. I came on out
and crossed the field, my presence scaring off
two short-fused rabbits bolting for their dens.

Foxes

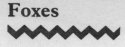

The beech leaf drums upon the sycamore,
the wood's splashed umber and scarlet, twilight
brings with it the floating cry of an owl,
an acorn popping from a cup alights

upon the swishing flick of a fast stream.
Sometimes I've heard the yapping peacock scream
of a vixen, or bark of a dog-fox,
announce the night, the moon a frosting gleam,

the air resinous with woodsmoke, leaf-rot,
damp tree-rime, bank moss. Once in the blue cold
a fox stood mucking out my garbage bin,
hunger had made his bloody instincts bold.

He vanished, sensing me at the window,
a farmer shot him in the poultry run,
the chicken jerking, its head bitten off . . .
He nailed the brush up as a russet sun.

Dissimulation's the art of the fox,
swimming downstream to ducks, sharp nose beneath
a raft of weeds, or lying on its back
playfully kitten-rolling on the heath,

feigning uninterest in the rabbits
it will grip by the neck, and skin alive.
Foxes climb trees, quarter a pastured lamb,
wallow in a mud coat, and then arrive

to tyrannize a foal hysterically,
they'll bite their leg off to escape a trap.
I shiver in the dark, a rabbit screams,
somewhere a collie's barking lends a map

to sunken farms, a fox is on the prowl,
engendering panic, moving unseen
through bracken, already paralysing
the rooster's head a snap will take off clean.

Rabbits

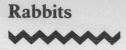

Rabbits the buffish-grey of scorched stubble
were bobbing into hill-sprints as my foot
opened the valley's silence – tinder leaves
crackling to a dry dazzle – a mulched soot

of powdered, sun-scorched humus underpinned
each footstep, leaves frazzled to a fine glass.
I waded through brambles, snapping bracken,
watching bunched tails flick through hairy oat-grass,

its panicled spikelets blotched with purple,
and came on down to where a warped cow-gate
was fashioned from a sawn-up rotting elm,
the bark rimed emerald. Twitchings of slate,

or a white powderpuff tail raised to run,
showed their deployment over a warren,
rabbits turned the colour of the landscape,
textured with the indigenous pigeon-

greys and roan-squirrelings of the hillside.
They'd stop and start, overfamiliar
with their territory, but gun-shy, quick,
camouflaged soldiers engaged in a war

of distinguishing sound from its intent.
I stood stock-still and they solidified,
inquisitive, sniffing, and when I moved,
it seemed my brain-cells had electrified

a corresponding fear-centre, signals
galvanized them into a breakneck run,
eyes big, adrenalized, wanting the dark
of their burrows. Behind me a red sun

cleared the dense chestnut wood, cows leisurely
ambled a meadow. Was it weeks later,
a full moon up, I heard a rabbit shriek
on the red fuse-end of a stoat's temper?

Voles

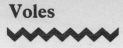

Tail-up, quarrelsomely industrious,
two bank-voles keep poking out of ivy,
their tremulous forepaws working to roll
a snailshell to their burrow, their beady

eyes, concentrated points of energy,
their rufous bodies ticking with power-lines
of nervous current; how the needle fangs
must have bitten grey flesh housed in a mine

a starling would splinter upon a stone.
Nimble, voracious, each renewed foray
conducted with prehensile whiskerings
showed greater caution; they would move away

as if disowning their quarry and freeze
at the least tremor. Bridged from stone to stone
a spider's web was built across the stream,
a red-eyed damselfly's audible drone

was negotiating waterpepper.
My staying must have sent them underground,
survivors from the short-eared owl, the stoat,
their presence dangerous in sunlight, a bound

would have them at the throat of their brother,
the short-tailed vole, screeching in a deadlock,
the victor slinking to a pool to wash,
its heart a piston jumping from the shock.

I moved downstream, the creatures of the night
had burrowed back to cave-darkness, a crow
was shouting from an oaktop, a farm-dog
chased a rabbit ten yards, then let it go.

On Fallow Foliage

after Hölderlin

It's there already in the grape,
the premonition of the wine,
it lives there like the shadow of a gold
earring on a woman's cheek.

Marriage must be for others,
how easily the calf in slipping free
becomes entangled in its chain.

You can count on it,
how the farmhand loves to stumble
over a woman fallen asleep
knitting a stocking in the shade.

His German mouth
which lacks all euphony
disengages from a brambly beard
and moves over hers
like a stream talking rain
in patters.

The Middle of Life

after Hölderlin

Commingled in one reflection
the wild rose and the yellow pear
map out their imprint in the lake,
and swans exalted by the calm
go by with silent wakes
or dip their arching heads
into the quiet water.

When winter comes, where shall I find
the summer flowers and the sunshine,
and where the shade the earth affords?
Unspeakably I fear the walls
debarring light, speechless and cold
the wind will find me out,
the weathercocks veer crazily.

Goldfish

Piebald-pebbling,
or black on scarlet, a tiger-lily,
orange of golden-rod or apricot,
they blow smoke-rings
across a lacquered pond and stealthily
back from a spot

the sun's fired red.
A damselfly fidgets on the green dish
of a water-lily, a dragonfly
flicks a blue thread
over the square-jowled browsing of a fish
lipping a sky

on which willows
are inverted green parasols. Crowfoot,
water-soldier and pink water-violet
flower in the glow
of yellow flags, a diving-beetle shoots
down through a let

in a surface
squiggled with the waterlights in satin.
I watch a shoal break into a whiplash,
a spiral race
that forms an arc, they have the glint of tin
in that jabbed flash

back to their slow
inert suspension, little buddhas prone
to meditating on a liquid sky,
or down below
brooding with the watersnail humped on stone,
they come to lie

  so comatose
they seem fixtured in the ice of cold blood.
Streamlined, poker-tipped, five in formation
   flush to a rose-
smoulder, passive, never portraying mood,
   their slow-motion

  advance across
the pond freezing to an embered halt.
They paint themselves into each new surface,
   fire-strikes on moss-
green canvases, tails erasing each fault
   without a trace.

Winter Mullet

The sun's berry-red in a ruck of blue;
somewhere, recalling Webster, a robin's
melancholy song is premonitory
of blade-edged ice, frost engraining its pins

into a field corrugated by cold,
the furrow-mounts crisp as a sheet of glass.
I make my way towards a coastal drop,
the water there's nursed by a powerhouse,

a tepid current that attracts offshoots
from the densely packed, spawning winter shoals,
wedged tight like overlapping slates, silver
of a flick-knife's punched out when a fish rolls.

These are the winter mullet, somnolent,
their world shrunk to the dimensions of trance,
they are unfeeling, semi-comatose,
their vision almost dead, their slow advance

that of someone flexing inside a dream
they can't connect with. I flick a flyspoon
tipped with white ragworm out towards the shoal,
and have it flutter, a jittery moon

working the shallows like a butterfly,
invites no quick uptake. Amnesiacs,
they're living with dulled instincts, one ungroups
and eyes the spoon, but hangs there, changing tack,

his metabolic rate too slow to chase.
Two or three basking in the warm stream shift
my bait, boxers prodding at a dummy,
they lip it back and forth, hoping to lift

the worm's flicker from the barb that they've sensed.
They disengage, their curiosity's
soon extinguished. In summer, they're playful,
dribbling a dough-ball round a float, or free

to shoot ten yards at a compulsive flash.
I stay on, the cold chaps my fingers red,
its pimpling's like dried beads of black hemlock,
the fish have tightened now into a head,

a mint destined to fall foul of seine nets.
Men keep a watch on these. A figure throws
a light over me in the early dark.
I jump to meet it, moth-dazed by the glow.

Bass

My feet slide on the downpour of shingle,
the shelf rattles like a line of bare teeth
chattering in the aftermath of shock.
Rain drives in; reefs show jagged points beneath

the swell; the cold's a razor on my cheek.
The surf keeps blasting, pushing back the stones
relentlessly, and neither will concede
their tireless protestation to go on

enduring, one insoluble, and one
reducible only over aeons.
I feel the wind walk through my little weight,
my feet wedged firm I fish the beach alone,

casting beyond surf on to shelving sand,
bottoming my green crab for solitary
bass nosing in to browse with the flood tide.
Late November, big fish rapaciously

feed with the storm prior to migration,
the cold has a mackerel's glitter, a glint
of blue and silver chasing. Where I cast
the wave's out-throw is granite, quartz and flint,

pebbles scoured mint-clean in the sooty dusk.
If I could place an ear beneath the sea
I'd hear the water running; the groundswell
could finger-spin a boulder crazily;

the fish are less pronounced in murk and not
the blaze of silver in a landing-net
scooping the played out, vibrant four-pounder
whose dash was for deep water. I reset

my bait; the wind brings with it stinging rain,
my world's constricted to a shuttered lamp,
here on a beach where the sea's jaws work hard
and stagger rubble into a wet ramp.

Worm

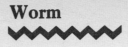

A freight-train pulling segments of himself
out of a dark tunnel, caution not stealth

defining his momentum; the earth's weight,
pit-propped by his spiral shaft is one state,

uncantoned, primal, and without a sun.
He works the surface of its sodden tons,

a bud-pink, stringy noodle veined with red
liverish hatchings, his bore-hole's his head,

the ooze of his tunnelling the liquid
churn of Verdun. Blind, he can't lift the lid

to see particulars sharp-edged by light,
the wiry fern's tooled serratures, the bright

jet of the starling's flashing eyes that stab
at the least earth tremor, the blackbird's jab

precise as a knife-thrower. What filters
into that planetless black's the flicker

of a running grassblade – the thrush's foot
shifting balance, its scale upon grassroots

the tinkle of a cymbal. Dark is law
in the worm's cellarage of drinking-straw

dimensions, turning the earth with a screw's
rotating friction, cold to the cold dew

in which assassins wait. To show a tip's
to be dragged writhing from the earth and slit,

engorged and dropped, whittled down for the snatch,
a bracelet that won't shut upon its catch.

Burying Beetle

Grass ticks with the punctuated rhythm
of someone busy with embroidery –

the underpinning of a green prism,
a water-emerald, diligently

combed and recombed by the tiny bull's horns
of the beetle's orange clubbed antennae,

its restless tracking's brought to scent the torn
carcass of a vole, blood has rouged an eye

in which the terror of its death's frozen
like something trapped inside a paperweight

to be released when the membrane's broken.
Now three or four are here to shift their freight

and bury it, maggotal carrion
in which they'll lodge their eggs, they tunnel down

beneath the matted corpse, their precision's
that of a team burying a razed town

to scrutinize it all in secrecy . . .
Their commotion's a landslide to the slug's

static adhesion, the red mulberry's
a bell-buoy cone to the ant-chain which lugs

a splinter up a slope. The glossy black
of funeral cars, these work to hide the spoil

their grubs will grow fat on, burrowing back
into decay; old bones profess their toil.

Ants

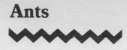

Ground-level scrutiny's what each convoy
    is versed in; on the march they are
like booted soldiers hand-picked to deploy

a valley-floor, their mandibles' fork-lifts
    manoeuvring the incessant
lava of boulders and felled trees that drifts

across their path. They map a region by
    their purposeful dexterity,
so low down that they never know the sky's

more than a puddled mirror they look in.
    Vehicular, quarrying loads,
their chain-gang tenacity is a thin

red fuse that flickers like a second-hand
    wavering between numerals.
They're earthquake victims dusted by white sand,

jockeying baggage from the seismic flaws
    of a city gone underground,
firemen able to ascend vertical

faces with a stunt-car's lurching motion.
    They simmer noiselessly across
a cragged flagstone in tank-drill or cushion

a dead beetle on a mobile rickshaw,
    their bodies square like elephants
beneath the victim's weight. Fast, quizzical,

their reconnaissance combs a territory
    and strips it of each utensil
serviceable to their massed colony,

autocrats of a starved third world. Close up
       their eyes are headlights, the thorax
wing-polished by a chauffeur, their stirrup-

roll affords high suspension. Grave-robbers,
       they swarm to an uncapped jam-jar,
and sugar-drunk, mark time in the larder.

Daddylonglegs

Stood vertical the body's a study
    for the anorexic thin-line
of a drawing by Giacometti,

the legs have a spider's retractable
    pyramidal apices when
squatting disoriented on a table,

its brittleness gone slack, the plump hump-back
    resembling an oxygen tank
grounded for fuelling. Gone dormant it lacks

knowledge of the closed, room-square dimensions
    the human's ill adjusted to.
Its quirky Wright brothers' aviation

leads to a frenetic arc. Dazed by light,
    its planet suddenly too close,
this one come in out of the autumn night

orbits a humming cone of gold that burns
    each renewed enmaddened assault
on its fixed station. Nightly it returns,

its wingspan fragile as a sycamore's
    green-winged halves of autumn fruiting.
Tonight its buckled stilts drag on the floor,

it can't levitate and its whirring runs
    crinkle like tissue-paper touched
by flame. It is the victim of a sun

that responds to a switch. I can't repair
    its intricate, vital damage.
It crackles like a comb run through live hair.

Drought

The cuneiform imprint of birds' feet dry
to dust scratched ensigns that the squatting fly

trembles in; its coal-black and royal-blue sheen,
a nervous ink-stain travelling between

the light and shade, pursues a figure eight,
and drops, a jutting nailhead in a gate,

sunning, then bulleting its martial drone
into a dried-up watercourse where stones

are snailshell patterned, and the stream's thorax
muffled with leaves. Its bed is a stone track

of unrolled freightage, unkempt as a coot's-
nest shored from whatever has lost its roots,

and forms a makeshift salvage. On the slope,
a sloe-eyed carthorse frisks a plaited rope

at the squalling cloud of darting horseflies,
their tiny iridescent lime-green eyes

sparkle like planets that have shrunk to beads.
Dust is the film that's paralysed the reeds,

and given the hillside a lion's coat,
an alligator's lentor. My glass throat

pumps with the rough farm cider's stinging tang.
I lie back hearing my pulse beat the clang

of a bucket on a wellshaft, and jump
up, head-down beneath a dry water-pump.

109

Blackberrying

The foxglove inclines by the blackberry —
a globe on which each country is embossed,
the craters are drought straits, dust-filled quarries

my eye works into, feeling the pressure
of mauve ripeness between finger and thumb.
I turn it up for inspection, unsure

of red and green pimplings, and watch a ray
of light distilled through Lombardy poplars
silver the peach sheen of the autumn day.

Here just last week a scarlet admiral
flickered like a black pansy on the fruit,
its delicate wings too ephemeral

to outlive the month. Now my fingers trace
design and symmetry of fruition;
the light's a goldsmith tooling in this place,

where sherry-coloured leaves quiver, a flick
and they rejoin the earth, a slow moulting
before the winds impose a flurried tick

of crisp drifts exposing galled undersides.
I listen on the outskirts of a wood,
the stillness is unnerving, magpies hide

in the elm tops and chatter as I mould
a berry to my finger, and the light
spins on my outspread hand a web of gold.

Red Geraniums

Pillarbox-red, blood-red, geraniums
flourished in dusty soil, garden beacons,
all head like a Scotch pine, and inclining
to a giraffe's bent-necked posture, these won

my trust as semaphores in the dry days
when even the marching ant turned khaki,
and the green bus's visigoth armour
battered through lanes with overhanging trees

to deposit me at the nearest farm . . .
Dog-days, two shirts a day, and alcohol
inducing instant sleep. Caught in mid-word
I'd startle with a parachutist's roll

to find the clock had jumped an hour, the heat
lit spitting cinders in the head, I'd watch
clouds burn off to vapour as they came in,
the countryside would blaze at a flipped match,

the gold bracken whipped to a tiger's skin . . .
Blue-headed, red-bodied, a hunting wasp
kept hovering by a hole in the wall,
the crackle of its flight, touchpaper-crisp,

its concave abdomen armour-plated,
one of the chrysids hungering to kill.
At intervals I'd hear the constrained roar
of a bull, tethered, fenced in on a hill

it would by weight of force have uprooted
and dragged into a landslide. Sometimes I,
camping in the huge brick ramshackle house,
would find myself flinching from the blue sky,

retreating deeper, dreaming of cellars,
of watershrews, of the fox's sunk hole,
the badger's tunnelled lair, the earth diggings
of the blind-eyed, snouting, nocturnal mole.

Violets

Their secrecy of place is matched by my
adjured concealment of that spot. Each year
I come back to it in the peach-red dawn,
the wood exhaling scents of after rain —
a dog's coat drying by a fire or stable air
warm with the bull. Almost I hesitate
to reach the green moss bedded round the roots
of ageing elms, and bend down to enquire
with tentative fingers of the mauve flower
shrinking beneath the arrow of its leaf,
a fragile concentration only shared
by those who seek it out, hermetic one,
its white spur opening to meet the shower.

Moors

Are unpredictable; the scraggy pelt
of an old farm dog gone grey in the jowls
with thistles, simpering from the raw belt

the wind drives, grudging in their sparse seasons –
heather will purple, and bushed gorse ignite
and baroque chasings of fern and bracken

turn rust-brittle in autumn, squirrel-red
interleaved with gold serrations. Their farms
are rooted in wind-breaks under a lead

sky smoking with rain, a chalk-dust of wet
that blows more persistently than the air
over the earth's face immovably set

in granite foundations. Out here the wind's
a fist squeezing man and bird back by force
of indentation, turning a crow round

in the daze of its skull, swinging a chain
that's worked off cliff-faced Atlantic breakers,
torrential in their seething. Wall and lane

are the only inroads into this range
that comes and goes with mist, a stubble mat
for elements that dynamically change

with the sea's turning. Up there man and space
are in true proportion, everything vast
and flying above a riveted face,

eyes polarized to take the whole scene in,
and reduce it to the grey of a pool
his mind can magnetize upon a pin,

and retain as a crystal light pours through,
but is scruffed up, mad-cap and blown downhill,
head over heels and panting at the view.

Horse Chestnuts

The wood was steaming with high summer rain;
grape-white, the light was filtered through the trees
so densely massed it seemed we stood beneath
a green cupola, so imperviously

interleaved, that the rain was gravel whipped
against a tarpaulin, the shuck of peas
unshelled into a bowl. We stood it out,
hearing with each increase a running sea

slowed by a shingle gradient, and then
in the pauses the big drops shaken down.
The leaves were donkeys' ears, long-pointed tips,
descending like a fountain from the crown,

their white candelabra flowers extinguished
with the month. The wood smelt of hop-sacks flushed
out of a barn, and airing in a yard.
We waited, anticipating the hushed

intervals between showers, caught up now
in the rain's drum-stick tapping, each crystal
a kitten advancing on cellophane.
Was it months later we returned, the fall

of green thorny-oyster pods, split open
to reveal polished nuts littering the ground,
spiny, the green of weed on wharf jetties?
What we had returned for was what we found,

a quality of underwater light,
this time diffused with amber and yellow,
a white sun pouring through interstices,
glinting, luminous, like a vein that flows

perennially through those branches, a light
that would map out the tree's shorn skeleton
in barest winter, and give to its shape
the hard, glazed dignity it would put on.

Baudelaire's Paris

General Cavaignac stands, his swan-white gloves
defiled by a single rose-thorn of blood.
He holds the stained one like a lint dressing
torn from a peasant choking in the mud

in the morass of Faubourg Saint-Antoine –
the bourgeoisie cleaned like a herring shoal,
my step-father surviving the pogrom,
his turkey paunch braided in its martial

arrogance, flushing out the mob the way
a pheasant's beaten from its hiding place.
An alligator choking on a corpse
is more edifying than his mauve face

spitting out the gristle of the masses . . .
The days of my revolutionary youth
cool like fuming lead ladled in a mould.
Now I sniff out the subtleties of truth

in every heightened sensory response;
the muse is a black angel or the white
phosphorescence of a travelling star.
I wander through the old Paris at night,

retracing paths I took with my mother,
those melancholy walks beside the Seine
observing silks, bad oil paintings, bookstalls,
a plum-blue mist dispersing into rain,

the barges lit up in the violet dusk.
Paris that harboured Villon and Racine
is rubbled, the old quarters shaken down,
and in the effluent sewer-rats preen

their glossy whiskers. I can smell the gas
of a new age steam from a muddy pool;
the patronage of the King's counting-house
has vanished, and the poet's left to cool

like Ovid in exile. Everywhere mean,
officious, grey-cuffed bureaucrats withhold
the bullion stashed for a poet's fist.
Hugo alone erects a tower of gold

from novels thick as the steps to the Louvre.
I roll on duckboards; the one sharp dandy,
patched up, shabby as a provincial priest,
sipping an ulcerous rot-gut brandy

at a table near the Folies Bergère.
The couples pass, old whores upon their beat,
their faces white as plaster of paris,
they angle whale-fat thighs from street to street,

enticing me to follow. Already
I sense the dripping stairs, the muted lamp
casting a red pool on the counterpane
holed with tobacco burns, the bedding damp,

a heaped lair where the cockroach multiplies.
Pride's like the stick that gives spine to a flower,
resolute. I concede neither to flesh
nor common taste, a camel needs no shower

to make its long trek through burning deserts.
My city, where Sainte-Beuve is domed in glass
like a stuffed toucan brought from the tropics,
and won't lift a finger to help redress

the execrations heaped upon my name.
Le poète maudit, balanced on a mound
yellowed by corpses, I can feel my luck
desert me, and take off like a greyhound.

The Irretrievable: Baudelaire

My heart's a cracked bell, I can trace its flaw
through seismic fissures: it harbours a snake
engorged on rabbits, birds, its dormant coil
electrified at each jolting earthquake

that rocks me like a skiff spun round and round
on a compass needle before it dips
into a vortex. I'm always outside
the engagement of my senses, life slips

corrosively through my inert channels
and silts my veins but I can't make it start.
Those long nights in Mauritius, I was free
to touch life's spinal chord not stand apart.

I still remember black thighs, and a fire
around which men danced shrieking, lifted high,
when the spirits came down to savage them.
The stars were diamond chips in a mauve sky,

so near I counted them; my welts still bled
from that rum-tempered sailor's whistling cat
that lashed me for my priggish arrogance,
I, the young dandy with his books and hat

and disinclination to know the sea.
I festered for days in the blinding heat
of my cabin, bored by the ocean's blue
spaces, and sudden squalls that rose to beat

us mastless round the Cape. The sailors clung
like ruminative spiders to the shrouds
and spindled back and forth at the sea's pitch,
for days we ran beneath an iron cloud,

and press-ganged into service I spat out
my venom, madly cranking a pump hoarse,
my head a fragile shell in which the wind
seemed trapped deliriously. My mouth grew coarse

as any sailor, but I wore white gloves
to protect the pristine gloss of my hands,
and waterproofed my books and opium stash.
I dreamt we'd founder on Circe's island,

and greet her troop of sailors on all fours,
hirsute, pig-snouted, snuffling for the cure,
to be converted back to human flesh.
Their legs and genitals chapped with heat sores,

their queen ripening in a silk leotard,
her thighs tattooed with cerulean peacocks,
a zodiac woven into her hair.
But what we sighted were only bald rocks,

snag-toothed, anfractuous in rings of swell
that boiled to a tempestuous Alp of spray.
I longed for cafés, whores, the Paris fog
smoking round barracks, or a calm blue bay

in which to swing in my hammock and dream
of the greater riches I'd left behind
in the Byzantine trappings of my den.
Voyaging disappoints us, it's the mind

that travels through the blizzard of the stars,
while we the victims of infernal dice
need strong stimulants to appease the flesh.
We're fastened to a trundling ball of vice

by a girl's slender ankle-chain. But now
it's land we sight, or the familiar
sea-sick mirage of those who've lost their feet.
Our ship slips like a panther through zoo bars.

Baudelaire's Abyss

Our brains are crucibles of Dante's hell,
we smell the leaking gas of our own death
like cabbage rotting in a sodden field,
its arsenic coats our blood, our camel's breath

filters from flues in which our brain-cells burn,
our souls cinder to Carthaginian pyres,
and yet we agitate those flames, liquor
and drugs and venery force-feed the fire

until we hiss with autocombustion
and ignite like a torch dowsed in petrol,
a red-hot poker rammed up Lesbia's bum . . .
We drizzle through life, prisoners on parole,

feeling in everything a mustiness,
each handhold's so impermanent we slip
from a trapezist's dizzy heights to that
cavernous hold in a becalmed slave ship

bound for Morocco with its freight of bilge,
in which we remorselessly gag for air.
The age has made the soul extinct, it hangs
bat-like in a zoo-aviary and stares

at fruit placed for its peculiar sickness,
it's like the last dodo in a tureen,
men eat rather than keep God's legacy.
Chemicals frazzle every square of green

that survives the new Paris. Block on block
aspires toward some terminal nightmare
of wards for the tubercular, or cells
in which the mentally ill sit and stare

at an uncut rigormortis of cards . . .
Our journey through the city's labyrinth
leaves us confused, drug-doped and envious
of the stability of those on plinths —

old generals weathering to permanence
in bronze or stone, while we stand nervously
on the edge of the void, birds with clipped wings
denied that turquoise rift where sky and sea

are indivisible. We're like insects,
and don't dare lift our eyes to shoals of space
resounding with their silent emptiness,
and when we look into a neighbour's face

for signs of comfort we encounter sties,
an ego encrusted with barnacles
of self-love, spidercrab-brittle, weedy
as though fished out of the black marsh of hell

to pump a red pulse in our diaphragms.
And you, Jeanne Duval, hennaing the grey
mop-haired straggles of your early decline,
left the void open when you lurched away,

your head fissured, a bottle in your hand,
wheezing through salons to a workhouse bed,
coughing a blood trail on the boulevard,
the blotches resembling a mulberry's red

unburdening of ripe fruit. What I hear
is a metronomic footstep beyond
the remotest visible star, a pulse
beating in the pit of a stellar pond

on some green archipelago of Mars.
I listen, we are frozen, minutes run
between our fingers like a waterfall.
My heart's a black swan climbing to the sun.

Baudelaire in Middle Age

Fear is a parasite whose increments
expand to a void both inside and out,
we wear its countenance like the red cross
slashed on a blighted elm crippled by drought,

and yet we're dropsical, a polyp sack
weighs like a bladder at our arid core,
its pustules file into our blood, we choke
beneath the heavy swipe of Charon's oar

and raise a blue face to the waterline.
It's glacial despite the stifling heat
that grizzles Paris to a carpenter's
pepper of sawdust. Couples in the street

sense how I peel the foreskin from their skulls
with the dexterity of a fish knife
handled by a mortician – a draughtsman's
clean edge autopsying husband and wife

on their restless stomp up La Rue Cadet
to the Casino. My frosted white hair
and holed suit pinched upon the skeleton,
my eyeballs, blown up to a lobster's stare

before the boiling cauldron fires it red,
attract averted eyes. I hear them speak
of me as a defrocked priest, a debauched
scatologist whose skin smells like a leek,

and who goes hand in pocket to Ancelle
to keep his blowfly creditors at bay.
Age is a birthmark branded by a snake's
whiplash, a pip that ripens to decay,

not with the measured metronomic tick
of the clockhand on the Chambre Correctionnelle's
pea-green wall where they ridiculed my book,
but with the electric jab of a bell

warning Nero Rome and his hair's on fire;
even one's lice atrophy and shrivel
to victims of vesicular famine,
a kind of green ooze mingles with one's smell,

and work, that groove in which we place our hand,
as in a vice, and tighten the thumbscrew,
becomes evasive, it slips like a fish
through eddies, leaving me to count the blue

moons scored upon my blotter, while the stair
creaks with some creditor's thug changing foot
with pins and needles. What can they salvage? –
no grave-robber's toothpick would find a boot

worth heeling, or a saleable work-sheet.
They sell *Les Fleurs du mal* in the junk heaps
along the quays, its parchment paper soiled
by smutty fingers. No jackal on heat

would find kindling-sticks in the jewel-cold blaze
that packs each sensuous image with snow.
Brushed by the wing of madness, I shiver
above a spiral shaft of vertigo –

the city's tiny, it's a matchstick maze,
its citizens are chain-ants thrumming by,
each with a mule-eyed passiveness. They slow,
and drowsing I can hear the wheedling cry

of a starved cat kneading today's letter
from *Le Figaro* declining my work.
I stand up dizzy like a man lifted
off his feet by the hangman's sudden jerk.

Baudelaire's *Aesthetique*

Cobalt, manganese-blue, vermilion,
the boy experiments with curlicues
and marbled whorls of colour, then stands back
in deference to Manet's truer blue

his hand can't vitalize, nor fix a light
into, his boy's thin modelling torso
toadstool-blotched with paint, as he slips the noose
around his throat, and at a single blow

sends the pin-legged chair crashing to the floor . . .
Cut down, his face is like the hectic cheese
Manet used as a first experiment,
colouring its green mouldiness to please

the captain of a mutineering ship,
the young artist watching each sea-mood change
its blinding iridescence with the sky's
troubled shoaling, learning how to estrange

then rebraid colour with such resonance
the pictorial action is poetry.
Manet, whose beard crackles like dry bracken,
whose misanthropic lips sarcastically

deplore an age that's fixed in wet cement,
its backward look into the grove of myth,
draws on the real, a city that's endowed
with the rind of the old, and the firm pith

of a new age, its neckties, polished boots,
its drinkers lobbing bottles in the Seine,
its whores' expression of lace petticoats.
And Delacroix his equal in disdain,

eloquent in his studio oratory,
maintaining that an artist worth his brush
should have a bird's reflexes to capture
and sketch a man's form in its downward rush

out of a window to the boulevard.
They shine as luminaries in the dark,
quick to perceive man's transience, his fall
the red flash of rose petals in a park

after the violence of a summer storm;
their studios designed for work, not stage-
trappings of armour, Malayan kukris,
old Gothic ironwork, things still the rage

with the plebeian, but excised by those
who see the real beneath the artefact,
the figure whittled down to a thin stem,
its floriated branchings useless facts

for the Salon's blunt-fingered exhibits.
Delacroix, who arranges his palette,
fastidiously as a flower girl,
conceiving how each tincture will transmit

a colour catching like a parrot-fish
flashing its rainbow in a clear grotto,
works all day obsessed by a change of light
he can't capture, then slips into the flow

of street life, hungry for the sparkling dice,
or gossip from his hare-lipped maid. The real's
the current we pick up on, laying waste
the marble blocking of a head to feel

a pulse describe the body's attrition,
or colour evoke music, as Chopin
conjured from Delacroix a brilliant bird
riding the abyss to the wind's slow spin.

The Treadmill: Baudelaire

〰〰〰〰

A tonsured porcupine, the poet's trussed
at the expense of fiction, Flaubert, who
ransacks a library shelf for a chapter,
working all day at swordpoint, then at two

extinguishing his lamp before the dawn
catches him sanguine, dressed in a tarboosh,
the drops of his moustache starched with coffee.
He looks like someone cut down from a noose,

his body stiffened, locked with elbow cramp,
his eyes the pink of tiny squids; his pen
a jeweller's instrument for polishing.
Not so the poet in his slummy den,

distilling to compress a hundred times
to salvage one unmarketable line.
The bourgeoisie divest us of laurels,
stoning us with invective, flushed by wine

that dilates the liver to a puffy
lamprey, left stranded, rotting on a beach . . .
Gautier and Hugo live by popular
fiction; the tritest narrative's a leech

to sentimental taste – I see them stacked
on Sainte-Beuve's desk, awaiting panegyrics,
his high forehead and batrachian face
working to extract bad-taste with chopsticks,

and prune each novel with a curate's eye.
He has a peasant's love of reticence,
a mind that thuds in a narrow furrow,
and when he praises it's for abstinence,

his plump hand clammy as a camembert.
The literati shoot like tame minnows
around a self-asphyxiating bowl,
their florid arabesques and rococo

verses have a flea's legs for scaffolding;
they die before we can locate the itch
of their ephemera, jettisoned leaves
crackling to black ash in an autumn ditch . . .

I keep the cool of a Tiberius,
inviting speculation, known to none,
irreproachably dignified, the head
of a sack-covered, boot-plastered icon

dragged once around the Field of Mars, declined
the very least of patronage. We drop
our lines into a dead incense-burner,
and listen for the whistling axe to chop

their tributaries at the roots. I fish
for editors with an unwilling bait,
preferring poverty to the mad *coup*
which smashed my book in one torrential spate

for less obscenities than Zola packs
into a chapter that survives the press.
A sickly, atrophied Normalian,
he floats above the stream like watercress,

resilient, determined to endure
the wash of his own anaemic reviews.
Already he scents the first pan of gold,
the novel multiplying to a new

civic mausoleum built tier by tier
on pulp, and flying the Republic's flag,
the idle bull-nosing forward to read
like carthorses occupied with nose-bags.

The Curved Hip: Baudelaire

Fleshed out, they terrify us; they retain
the iridescence of the dragonfly's
cerulean sheath, for less than the instant
we hold them transformed, women gone like flies

to oil their colours on the trout-stocked pool.
I see them through a glass; the indigo
of a blue-skinned nymph like the god Shiva,
turning vermilion and then the sloe-

black of an amazon with a geisha's hips
and the slim torso of a boy. My nose
still hungers for the scent of mother's clothes,
her lace, satin and fur, and the pink rose

of her trembling underthings. As a boy
I'd unstopper each perfume phial, and make
a palette of my wrists, mixing each scent
until it dried into a fragrant lake

and blazed like dry sticks crackling on a heath.
At night I saw my mother's ivory
body turn to a firefly's brilliance
of burnished jewels; fear kept my memory

forever vigilant at her keyhole,
a schoolboy reading Racine's *Bérénice*,
dreaming of couches heaped with ostrich plumes,
and mad emperors showering pearls like peas

at the enmaddened mob. All flesh eludes
the form that we would have it take, its mask
dulls like the scales on an expiring fish,
we're left stranded upon a rolling cask,

resisting the pressure of a whirlpool . . .
A sou for Jeanne Duval, half a night's board
in a bordello, she who lay captive
upon my rug, tied up in silken cord,

while I ran rubies and sapphires over
her body, teasing her until she caught
them in her lips and spat them on the floor.
I'd watch her mood change to a storm, her taut

sinews working to unleash a bush-fire,
then I'd retreat, and leave her combustion
whipcracking round the room, a smelting iron
that wouldn't cool, until each silk cushion

was lacerated by her shredding nails,
a candle jetting flame on the carpet . . .
What we begin in excess, ends in drought,
a kept woman turns from an idle pet

into a lion couched down in the grass,
waiting to hang its fury on the side
of a lame-tired zebra. For nights I'd have
to take refuge outside Paris, or hide

in hotel attics, frozen, impotent,
dreaming of a woman who'd offer all
but the meshed interlacing of her thighs.
It's the wet days of childhood I recall,

a cortège filing towards Montparnasse,
the women with their scented handkerchiefs,
quiveringly upright despite their loss,
and raindrops scoring the first yellow leaf

splashed on the rimed plaque of a family vault
entwined with white triton flowers of bindweed.
That mood seemed permanent, a compassion
beyond all reach, satisfying a need.

Going Back

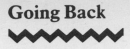

They spring up like round pennywort
proliferating in the lane –
faces dragging with a carp's beard,
scaled with age, tight-lipped with disdain

that an intruder's jumped the falls
into their green provincial pool –
its feudal tench and pike still browse
on rotting algae and distil

an odour of rising tear-gas . . .
I stand and smart. These seasoned shoals
of invincibly doctrinal
Methodist preachers on atolls

are singed by their unsparing fire.
Glutted with morals, they are clams
choking on their own ingestion.
Their paunches sag with fry; they jam

the unrepentant till they break . . .
A small town, I skirt its edges,
tail-up, an alighting magpie
seeking the shelter of hedges,

nervously gone at a shadow . . .
Sanctuary's never a home town,
nettled with parochial intrigue,
its laurels, senate and gold crown

melted down in a boiling pot,
its monuments lichened with rust,
its clockhands stuck immovably.
I move upon a fragile crust,

beneath me creeper-roots ensnare
the way forward; no scythe or hoe
could lop the green weeds from this ditch;
the bailiff ploughs his own furrow,

one foot in politics, one land.
I stoop to a stream's energy,
pure, unpolluted, torrential,
its cooling points to the way free,

water that's both clear and neutral,
its only motive to advance.
I cup it in my hands and drink
fragments of sky caught in its dance.

Kleptomaniac

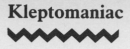

My eye's a magnet for my hand,
prismatically it groups the things
I need but do not understand,
silk scarves, sunglasses, perfumes, rings.

What brings me here's an obsessive
desire to appease a whirlpool
whose current quickens. I arrive
at theft before my mind can cool

the calculation of my hands.
I'm marked, but uncurtailed, someone's
always behind me when I stand
deliberating on the one

object that multiplies before
my index of adrenalin
plummets. Even outside the door
my eye keeps catching on a pin,

and I return, unsatisfied,
my topcoat pockets stashed with loot.
Whatever restraint I had tried
to impose is removed, my foot

hums on an accelerator.
There's always one whose impartial
absorption's not a customer's,
his hands don't fit the crystal ball

he toys with, his deft strategy's
to watch my moves from his blind-side,
that lizard-like dexterity
with which my fist withdraws to hide

a weight that's alien, hardly warm
from contact with my skin. Replete,
my movements are diffident, calm,
I make no arrow for the street,

but linger with the crowds, aware
arrest won't come until I leave,
when someone's vice-lock grips me where
the suede patch frays upon my sleeve . . .

Today I'm safe, I've slipped the scent,
the store detective's like a stoat,
a student squatting down has bent
a brick-sized book inside his coat.

Heirloom

Your mouse-grey 1950s obstinate
Morris Minor, would wait upon the hill,
a battered perennial amphibian,
sheeted on coastal roads, driven until

its wear seemed contemporaneous with yours,
its interior smelt of wintergreen-
embrocation, it was your reading-room,
a snail's house slanted on a height between

two oaks and a mushroom-domed mulberry.
The sea beneath was like the turquoise eye
in a peacock's feather, or wintry grey,
slammed in the hollows, while an opaque sky

had lights come on like small aquarium fish
flickering in shoals round the coast. You read
for hours there, the thrillers of your youth,
the writers still alive, their novels dead.

That car bequeathed you by a friend was your
most intimate possession. Its headlights
were an ophthalmic frog's eyes, and its brakes
defied all but a tightrope walker's slight

response of pressure; you were the master
of an eccentric mechanism none
dared disattune. Often I'd trace your car
come out of a tunnel into the sun,

late autumn sunlight, and tick round the coast,
labouring the hill to this sheltered eyrie,
where gulls hung still, then lurched at a tangent
over some object imperceptibly

thrown up by the wave. Now that car is mine,
garaged after your death, its engine mute.
I walk back to your parking-spot, the waves
climb the rock-face and vertically salute.

Regular

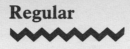

One of a kind who finds sanctuary here,
withdrawn, pacing your drinks, circumspectly
dressed in a graphite pinstripe, your black eyes
sunk like a hamster's were an inventory

of small particulars, a pub's archives
impressed upon your mind's engraving-plate,
so many years spent watching on a stool . . .
Aloof, unfamiliar, you'd hesitate

over your choice of drink rather than have
the barman come to know your preference
between Johnnie Walker and Haig. You held
the liquid in your glass with deference

for its gold-spot of volatility,
and added water as though refilling
a deoxygenated goldfish-globe.
The admixture clouded, a tarnished ring

gone copper from the march of verdigris;
and if the liquor's burning took you where
you saw things double or in a vortex,
you remained dispassionate, a fixed stare,

inscrutable, conceding no gesture
of approbation or contempt. No one
intruded on the stool you'd ironed out.
You faced the bar like someone who has won

the right to be recognized, but ignored,
an oxygen plant drinking all the air,
so that the others laboured breathlessly,
contracting in a ring. Grease on your hair,

bootblacked its natural grey. You were a dog
begging acceptance, swallowing your bark,
following an invisible keeper
out of the swing-doors into the pitch dark.

Cornering

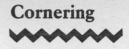

A hut puddled by sunlight mellowing
to amber from its jacinth source, and you
leafing tessellations of photographs
ordered into a sequence on the blue

air-force blanket daisied with ash-droppings,
nekton, or are they sun-burst shooting-stars
blown earthwards like a planetary pollen?
That one of moths dispersing as a car

overtakes the lens, shows the driver's eye
pinned inwards, focused upon an image
which cannot be recomposed twice the same.
His snouted gesture suggests quiet rage,

he cannot steer thought round this one crystal
which proves insoluble, its blue flashlight
bubbling like a police car's stalled in traffic.
These shots are your inventory of the night,

fixtures that killed time at a lit moment,
banking it on a reel you sensitize
to a frozen condensation of speed.
It's unconscious, I say, you hypnotize

before the shutter clicks the way a cat
has paralysed the bird before it leaps,
and on the instant of fastening, unthaws
the bird's mind sealed in a premonitory sleep

in which all sound's turned off, the garden dead.
I go outside and cross a field to where
a road ribbons through scutched with pimpled treads;
the light hangs off, a dusty solar flare

catching the corn-ears in a yellow flood.
Your eye can't see me level with a gate,
concentrating on detail, unopposed,
to butt the air without a duplicate.

At Midnight

It wasn't death that brought him to the door
that night when a black-out had candles glow
in solitary farms, and on the floor
one's feet interrogated things the way
a diver does, so apprehensively
one seemed to kick on upward and away.
What I remember is his standing there,
his tongue a nervous fish inside a jar,
his eyes not looking, but pooling their stare
between his feet, a withheld urgency
transmitted through each nerve, and like a hare
he shook, too frightened yet to speak, the dark
behind him that he kept pointing into
was lit by something burning, a crashed car . . .
We summoned torches, and in heavy coats
ran out into the night and icy stars
were spotting, bright fish jumping in a lake,
and found the car turned upside down, aflame.
One pair of bloody footprints led from there,
the others pointed back the way we came.

The Meaning

Lozenges of light shimmer through the beech,
the green is vegetal, a man stoops down
examining strawberries beneath bird-nets,
last winter's pumpkin has turned soggy brown,

his cantaloups and scarlet-fleshed melons
have prospered, watered snow beneath firm rinds,
and coral-pink sweet-williams show white
centres of Tudor lace, while sweetpeas wind

their shell-pale inflorescence around sticks.
The man's disquieted, three centuries
have elapsed since the Fairfaxian oak
was counted foremost amongst Marvell's trees –

the lawn a mirror at Appleton House.
He leans back in the shade, this chosen spot
has served him well in a fraught century,
he's learnt to concentrate upon this plot,

to diffuse nerve into pure energy.
He's parked his car above the slope, its blue
metallic bodywork heats in the sun,
a wing dent's knocked its symmetry from true

to a worn hunter's trophy of chipped chrome . . .
He steadies, one hand sheltering his eyes
against a light that simmers as it falls
and stays down there around his feet; he tries

to find a meaning in the afternoon,
a permanence beyond the simple toil
of tying netted fruit trees to the wall,
the past has blood-roots in his nurtured soil,

yet work it as he must, he is detached.
It's off somewhere where light glazes a hill
that life points to connectives which aren't here.
He feels that energy by standing still,

and redirects it to a fluid shape
that's composite, man bending with the light,
following its arc. Three centuries back
blood stained this ditch from stragglers lopped in flight.

Bar Stand

Your glottal drawl, a sailor's boom,
its timbre seasoned by alcohol,
audible a pitch higher than
the crack that made that small man roll

with tears he couldn't sober.
Always you must hold the pivot
to the conversation's kilter,
forcing tongues by cap and spigot

house-rounds to defer to you,
your hands spread wide on the counter,
your stoop felling your proper height,
and not just here but in them all,

a regular when you enter
on your incessant village rounds –
Suffolk to the Essex border,
well lit in each new stamping-ground,

pinkies, whisky or tequila,
amiable and jocular
with a seaman's itinerary
lending you an oracular

note to parochial affairs.
What's a village but a Chekhov
story, or a roulette table?
All the faces must turn up,

be scrutinized and reassorted,
some in different beds, and some
scandalized, then tarred and feathered.
Each head here's a turnip man.

Always you'd assume your role,
bending low to steer the talk
into a pool you'd regulate,
they the blackboard, you the chalk,

still seeking a captive ear
two hours after closing time,
parrot-eyed and squinting now,
a self-parody, self-mime.

Home meant trusting to your instincts,
ninety on dark unpoliced roads,
startling a village coven
consorting with the woodpile toads.

Smoke on Water

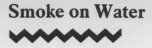

A tug churns in the offing, its coot-black
buffeted boot-shape treads the swell down flat,
its chugging's audible and a seahorse
of smoke curls from the funnel. Harbour rats

keep sleekly bristling by a sewage pipe.
The water's syrup with a peacock's tail
of floating oil outbrilliancing the sky.
Inshore a man stands watching a red sail

flicker down-wind. If he has time to kill,
he wears the doubt upon his face that shows
the stress of a puzzle he can't resolve.
He looks like someone counting flakes of snow

who grows more confused with each new flurry . . .
I stand and watch him. On the South Pier side
lorries are stacked with timber, and dredgers
keep slogging out to sit squat on the tide

and detonate the seabed. The man shifts
position and suns on a packing crate,
his head hangs unsupported, and he seems
caught in the drift, not opposing the spate,

but now a part of it as ripples flow
converging in the current's arrowhead.
He blends in with the backdrop, and I see
nothing to distinguish him but the red

socks visible beneath trousers gone high.
The man's the purpose for my staying here,
I'm linked to him by some magnetic pull,
my puzzling out his confusion makes clear

my need to recognize my own, and how
a common clouding shadows the clear source
we live in, creatures trapped in a rock pool,
seeking shelter before we regain course.

The Wake's Departure

They're going home: headlights flare gold across
a farmyard, startling a grey nuzzling rat
into a straw pile; some have edged the weight
of a coffin's underside on shoulders
of suits so rarely aired they hold their crease
like a cricketer's whites. Lit by toddies,
even the moribund are jocular;
the body consigned squarely to its ditch,
the talismans divided, the estate
a widow's roof-leaking thatched usufruct.
They've placed his Sunday hat upon the gate.

A Girl in Summer

Your hair hennaed a blazing marigold
was a flickering fireball through the trees,
your girl's body pinched to a boy's torso
pronounced its shape through army dungarees,

an ornamental cartridge-belt circling
the thin hoop of your waist. No amazon
exercising a spear-arm, scorched bark-black,
sizzling by the verminous Thermodon's

steaming fetor of gnats, but someone drawn
half by the sun and half a lime tree's shade,
sunning warily, only disturbed by
the constant sorties of a squirrel's raid

on remnants of a picnic, then its bolt,
the crackle of fire running up a tree . . .
I chose a horse chestnut's dense canopy,
its green light a flickering undersea

I looked up through as a diver that's hit
bottom and seeks for contours in the haze;
the milling leaves were a teeming whirlpool.
And if I lost sight of you in the maze

my eye was led into, you resurfaced
in the foggy interior of a bar,
your eyelids the pink of the dicentra's
heart-shaped locket flower, your eyeballs stars

that flashed like raindrops on a trembling leaf,
and formed two hazel pools I fished upstream,
frightened to smash my fly impetuously
on the run's white arrow gusting to steam,

but angled obliquely, missing my cast,
placing it wide, then waiting for the catch,
while you jumped up alarmed at the ashtray's
popping hecatomb lit by a flipped match.

The Deep End

The wine I drank was pack-ice in my head,
my balance rolled on duckboards polished by
the treacherous green algae's mirror-slide . . .
I shivered as the dawn's salmon-pink sky

erupted over the bay, a scarlet
sun still obscured by slate massings, a cold
light adding herring scales to the skyline.
The torchlight picking out my steps was gold

streaking over the forbidden causeway
to the jetty's deep end. I squatted there,
my rod unpacked, spooning groundbait into
the tidal calm, mesmerized by the glare

that oiled the waters, waiting for the first
quicksilver roll of a mullet's belly
to pronounce the shoal had picked up the scent.
Danger kept me alert, my truancy

from the sleeping house, my fishing the deep
proscribed by my father's admonition –
a child who couldn't swim risking the tide's
octopus of currents, apprehension

magnified my each move to diamond-point.
Like the mullet, subterfuge was my art,
I empathized with their nervous browsing,
their liquefaction, the drum of my heart

seemed amplified to carry round the cove . . .
Always I feared a stranger at my back,
the voice reproving, the indictment harsh.
I fished the tide till it flipped on its back,

lazily receding; the jetty edge
was an anvil-face of blue scale glitter
dried to an iridescent paste. I stole
back from that secret place, my feet feathers

that hardly brushed a stair in the still house.
I'd grown adept at withholding my weight,
each footstep came down on a ball of wool,
perfect in its timing, deliberate

in its subtraction of a boy's clay-feet.
I balanced as one standing on a cliff,
warding off the deep end, surprised this time
by father waiting, spine-up, poker-stiff.

Behind the Scene

Alignment's hardest, it's the billiard's cue,
we mentally perceive, but can't effect.
Words won't come right ways up when down's their due,
approximate again, we reselect,

nose down, beating out the elusive prey
we can't transfix but narrow to a track
where it's least guarded and can't shy away.
If it doubles on us we startle back

like someone withdrawn from binoculars
who has trouble adjusting to the glare.
It doesn't pay to get familiar
with where the poem could lead, the mad stare

of the red-eyed wolf-daimon's glowering prowl's
sufficient to lead on to that black pit
where blood's a lustration to those who howl,
and shades are moths inside the cave and flit

from wall to wall. But once seen, always known,
what nags upon the thread must be retrieved,
and scrutinized beneath a lamp, alone,
uncertain if the act will be reprieved

by darker forces. Rilke thought that ten
good lines in a lifetime are all we get.
Transmitting signals over a blank page,
the poet feels the tightening trap that's set

to lock him fast, and telescopically
narrows in, distracted, a fly-swatter
beating a bull's horns, nipping scotch early,
enmaddened, whizzing his glass to shatter.

Stamping Ground

At night the sibilance of rain in wheat,
and in the pauses crickets, a strayed cow
bellowing from beneath the alder hedge,
a charged mosquito policing the window,

a book picked up three times before the dawn
redly shivered through arrow folioles
of Lombardy poplars, and the green east
took on the plumage of an oriole.

A night, a day, and what's familiar here
has to be relearnt, I see near things, far.
The signposts have been altered, cuneiform
hieroglyphics, they point towards the stars . . .

But look again, on every side a farm,
couched in the shelter of a hill, defines
its durable three centuries of granite.
The rain's given that stone a pinkish shine,

but only two are farmed, a swimming pool's
an oval turquoise cabochon in one,
a Rolls is stabled in the extant barn,
another year will see another gone . . .

Heat-haze, mistings, and now the cows deploy
across a meadow, ponderously slow,
bugged by gadflies, rooting whatever's green,
they walk with the weight of four men and tow

the dragline of a chain. I start my search
to redefine a place, a field, a hill,
the cars are red and black and blue beetles
scurrying to elude a raven's bill . . .

Up on the hill I find it, a fuzzed sea,
the surf roller-skating into the bay,
each white crest having crossed the Atlantic
with winds behind it from the U.S.A.

In and Out

Indoors, dispensable utilities,
the glint of car-keys, a bracelet of change,
papers, credentials, an identity
I've grown accustomed to, and yet I range

over the particulars of a life
with such quizzical incredulity,
I seem an intruder, a bright eye-lens
polishing facts for a biography,

he lived here once, his eccentricities . . .
Outside the purple lythrum's needle spire
ranges beside the blue globe-thistle's ball
bees electrocute to a crackling fire,

the lily's a science-fictional ear
able to record sound binaurally,
a de Graaf strain with a martagon's shape,
the fiesta-hybrid pendulously

strings stamens from its red sealing-wax throat.
I go back inside, detail here's less sharp,
my pen-nib activates the universe
I select from; a spider plays a harp

in a ceiling fissure, the gold strings hum . . .
I go from room to room preoccupied
with the diadrom pulse of poplar leaves,
and how the shifting cuckoo has replied

to its own echo all the afternoon.
Wind in the ash tree forms shadow canoes
leaved across a table by the window.
Why should all insubstantial things review

themselves in planes of light? My mind won't throw
a reflection; I know of it through words,
the endless permutations of a phrase
mapped out by the black-inked feet of a bird.

Writing a Novel

Co-ordinative pressure on the keys –
the stream of liberated ribbon runs
under the punched indentation of thought.
Each type-head is the trigger of a gun,

it fires precisely through a chafed black stream.
The plot thaws then backtracks into a blue
congelation of midwinter pack-ice.
I face the dazzle, sneaking into view

a woman bolts from a car, her white shoes
discarded as she runs across a beach,
red poppies twinkle on cerulean
when her dress lifts; she leans forward to reach

the crisp, flooding insurgence of the wave,
and stands, skirt hitched up, staring out across
the smoky-blue of the Adriatic.
The left spool halts, then inches back its loss.

Flow and counterflow, now I see the man
impatiently locked in his car, one hand
drumming persistently upon the wheel.
His dark glasses cast shadows on the sand,

he sees the world monochromatically,
vexation cuts a twist into his lip.
She's hardly visible running the wave,
outpacing the supine crawl of a ship,

the Lido's beach-parasols are pansies,
the sand's a mica-glint of ivory.
He drops a contact-lens and curses her
departure, lost from sight, now wave-struck, free

to meet the future where it coincides.
These are minor characters, a sub-plot
the ribbon maps out, a hound on the scent.
I leave her running on a string of dots . . .

The Music of Blue

for Maritza

If there's a colour to contemplation
then there's a music too if we could hear
beyond the word eluding us, for air
is resonant with notes that disappear
on our awakening, much as the flare
of a blue match-flame turns invisible
when held up to the sun. Mallarmé's fear

was that the blue was untranslatable,
and words were quartz crystals that wouldn't flow
but interfaced themselves. Yet blue is sheer,
demanding we brush it like the swallow
with quick wing-beats, for that altitude's clear
both in the passage out, and the return,
there is a blue above the grey below.

Gradations of cerulean engage
the eye in distinctions, for water keeps
no constant hue, and I could name fifteen
subtleties of sea-green and grey that meet
on a sea horizon, blues that are green,
and how a brilliant turquoise turns cobalt,
or becomes a sultry ultramarine

as clouds compose and recompose the sky.
There's challenge here above a shifting bay
of luminous sky-lakes; such flux demands
a music that is neither blue nor grey,
but isolates all colour in one band
of light, energy fired in a crystal,
as sunlight strikes on a lit cove of sand.

Mastery of the blue means equipoise,
if vision clarifies with depth we need

motion to create resonance, the two
maintained as dynamic antitheses
create those atmospherics of true blue
that give the poem mood, as a sad man
might walk here in rain, and colour the view.

We must forever like the sea-jade sky
be moving into a new quality
of light, intent upon a music known
in the wake of migratory swifts, and see –
their arrow strains towards a hidden sun,
composing clear notes for our memory
to reassemble when those birds have flown.

Pact

The eyes are bloodshot, stringy with the fleck
blearing the eyewhites of a flogged race-horse,
a current simmers, the pulse overshoots,
re-rounding the churned surface of a course

in which the rival is an outsider
who never shows – one gap in twenty trees
something's discernible, a billowing
of light blown back, an articulacy

of hooves hammered into clear syllables,
ordered, re-ordered, crisscrossed in black ink,
the line no sooner minted than reshaped.
The pact's remorseless, all night on the brink

of unhinged reason, I've faced a scored page,
a gypsophila of effaced birds' feet
fretting back to the tideline from margins,
each new jab questioningly incomplete;

although the furrow's clear, I know its track.
And it is always so, this need to burn
thought into that especial energy,
the scales unsilvered, powder in the urn . . .

the line set quivering, the music clear,
as suddenly the outrider's restrained,
and steers the tired hand with fluidity,
and with relief the tugging bit's contained.

Apprehension

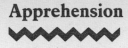

Mist as an apprehension, standing off,
all day the drag of boulders in the cove
worked through the poem's rhythm, pebbled words
resisting a groundswell,
buoyed up by the bright fibre of a thread
anchored to an invisible margin.

In the lane, a girl with red
Cornish hair jack-knifed an ivy cluster,
the berry-mace of blackheads
tinged purple. Was it thunder
clicked like two grating stone-blocks overhead?

A sign and then another sign,
the poem involved, picking out a course
with the fidgety pincers of a crab,
its legs enmeshed in twine.

Then at midnight the window open wide,
a ship lit up and standing off the coast,
the ticking snowflake of the Lizard light
pittering on the pane, I felt the thread
strum taut, resistant, holding in the night,
its owl-eyes bright, and staring red.

After Horace: Epodes 12

‍‍‍∿∿∿∿∿∿

Quid tibi vis
We both of us nurse a climacteric,
old courtesan you slap lubricious thighs
coaxing some elephantine paunch to screw,
cajoling me with your nepotistic
favours, your presents of watered-silk ties,
but I can smell the coot's-nest bushed beneath
each arm, the three-weeks-old make-up that flakes
like peeling stucco from your face, the wreath
of undyed hair that constantly escapes
the carrot henna. Rivals in old age,
you mock the earthworm slackness of my cock,
yet claim I manage Inachia each night,
flattening her bedding to a surfboard . . .
May any Lesbia who scorns my sex,
whose fingers are blackberried from the dye
of Tyrian purples, remember my groin
was once the platform of a mountain tree,
and even now my semen ducts run dry,
morosely marking time in a beer-hall –
my lust will gain me fairer prey than you
chalking up lewd sophistries on the wall.

Catullus 29

~~~~~~~

freely adapted

Mamurra's in discredit; only hands
who deal on a card-table, or incite
a map to redden when their feet can't stand
from some tyrannical debauch, condone
this tycoon's burning up of British coin,
his pinching the Gaul's carcass to the bone.
Puffed up with martial braid, gold-powdered hair,
he stalks from bed to bed, his appetite
keeps his fagged body grinding half the night,
this white dove, who presents a parody
of Adonis, stands pissing out his grape,
the liquid gold he got by pillage, rape,
his inheritance blown, so too the loot
lugged from the Pontic, and gold panned from Spain.
Why maintain him? This sycophant would bribe,
screw, steal, embezzle, sell Rome to the dogs
for a night's profligacy. Here he struts,
one of a breed, in soft Parisian boots,
who scatter Rome's wealth to the wind, and cheer
to see a great city razed to its roots.

After Horace: Epodes 14

Mollis inertia

Your petty triumph, Maecenas, pivots
on knowledge of my apathy that spreads
like ivy round an old oak stump that's dead.
My unwritten epodes receive the boot
of your indignation. I drowse as one
drugged on the toxic potions of green Lethe.
I juggle fragments, there's no lightning flash
to make my kite-grounded iambics run
for home. You say Teian Anacreon
dealing out facile metres for a lyre
was also struck dumb by the frustration
that raged in him for a Samian youth.
I see that you too are scorched with a fire
such as turned Troy into a blazing rick.
I smoulder on the page, stung by desire
for my new slave and his snake-climbing trick.
His flautist's fingers play upon my prick.

Nero

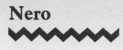

Is it so terrible a thing to die? –
Exile's a termite to the intellect,
one's lines resound against an empty sky
on some craggy outpost where goats dissect
a clifftop for a mouthful. None are spared,
even the household gods have rubbled heads,
the shrine of Vesta's defiled, and thunder
rumbles its omens over every bed.
Two-headed offspring, lightning bolts, a snake
a woman gave birth to, still dribbling red,
its markings interfaced with jewels, predict
the impending whirlwind we live under,
scattering Rome's twenty-one district plots
into a smashed mosaic, in its wake
a cone of fire spins to avenge this spot.

Matricide stains his bad blood with worse blood.
Agrippina, who curled upon her couch
enticing him to take her in a flood
of youthful frenzy, only had him touch
her pythonic hips through diaphanous
veils exposing her naked to her son.
He had her butchered, Britannicus too,
last of the Claudians, a brother done
to death, his gizzards shrivelled up in flame,
the whole deranged, effete imperial zoo
looking on, Burrus with his crippled hand,
Paris squawking, the eunuch retinue;
they buried him that night, even his name
was omitted from the ribald statue.

Men fear the streets at night, the drum-skin throb
of Nero's bacchanalia. He ties
his victims up in bearskins, and the mob
assaults them, gobbing spit into their eyes.

Poppaea rules his couch but cannot stem
a lust for every perversion; he rules
by virtue of Seneca's diligence,
a man whose austere philosophic school
accrues to it more riches than the state.
I envy Suillius his penitence
and soft Balearic exile; no poet
can publish, the Emperor has preference
over Lucan, my pine-enclaved estate
is eaten up by his indifference.

Our Empire cracks like worn crocodile skin,
it is a fishnet full of holes that flaps
at frontiers; Gauls, Frisians and Parthians
slough through the army's unprotected gaps.
Only in Britain does the eagle fly,
Suetonius licked a wild barbaric ruck
of troops marshalled by women – not a head
was saved – thousands stared from the horse-churned muck,
the smoking welter of a lashed rabble,
Boudicca's skin booted the blue of lead,
and yet that country's an untamed thicket,
its forests resist our tapemeasure roads.
Today our drill's the anaemic babble
of men who sit squat as paunch-bellied toads.

The model ivory chariots on his board
are playthings like the laurel that he wears
to face his golden statue with its bored
expression. Twenty times his height, it stares
towards the ceiling's fretted ivory.
The tyrant in the Golden House who sweats
beneath the lead weights placed upon his chest
for better respiration to abet
his vocal chords. His husky voice can't range

to the empyrean and when he rests
he wears a robe embroidered with gold stars.
Rome's become an international exchange
for gladiators, charioteers, mock wars,
there's not a statue's head that doesn't change.

His eye's his mirror, not a mirror stares
from the imperial rooms, in case she shows,
the dead mother who drags him by the hair
from sleep and suffocates him by a slow
immersion in an ant-hill. Nothing quells
the raging insomnia that has him run
tilting at statues, the amphitryon
of ransacked Greek gods, naked in the sun
that finds him rocking the gold statuette
of Victory, placed by the horn of Ammon;
the Red Sea's dredged for pearls to spot his room.
Whoever marries him must thread the net
of red and purple he throws at the moon –
Octavia died, a blade in her gullet.

The fire that gutted Rome, fanned by a wind
that stoked the blaze to a red tidal wave,
was at his instigation. In their minds
men have already placed him in a grave
the crow struts over. Things are upside down,
gold sand for wrestlers comes in place of wheat,
naumachias demand monsters from the deep
to be salvaged by a carnival fleet,
Africa and India scoured for beasts
smashed up like firewood – the Emperor can't sleep,
so must be entertained until the sand
in the arena's troughed with blood. He feasts
on peacocks encased in goldleaf, and stands,
divine exemplar of the human beast.

177

Profanation of every rite decrees
an inauspicious death. Men drown their words
like stones; each week a new conspiracy's
unearthed, the plotters killed before they're heard,
their heads are packed into an apple-bin —
even Seneca's had to renounce life,
his riches the Emperor's gratuity.
In Rome it doesn't pay to be a wife
who mourns a husband for she joins his pyre:
our only common law is treachery.
Paranoid, flanked by Mazacian horsemen,
nibbling aphrodisiacs to refire
his spent member, the song-bird in his den
thinks only of night. Lust heats like a wire.

Tyrant follows tyrant on thinning ice,
and each at last plunges to the black pool
to solidify. New taxes, new vice,
supersede before the old corpse can cool.
Nero, deserted by the army, ran
to some outlying villa, unprepared
for death, dusty, his silk clothes burred with thorns,
his unskilled sword-hand trembling and his scared
eyes appealing for respite. It took two
hands to assist him with the knife, his torn
windpipe gouting blood. The mob would have flayed
him alive, trussed and pitched him in a sack
into the Tiber. Now Galba's arrayed
in purple, men wish the old tyrant back.

Height: average, rarely used to good effect,
the body pustular, pitted with sores,
the features without singular defect,
but epicene, profuse sweat in the pores.
Eyes sea-blue, dwarfed by pupils, myopic,

neck squat on a pepperpot torso,
belly already slackly protuberant,
legs spindly, hair dyed gold, the voice a slow
drawl quickly mounting to hysterical
passion, eyelids pasted with indigo.
Histrionic, his one pursuit pleasure,
facetious, inordinately jealous,
hell-bent, I itemize his faults to cure
the harsh exile of one Sosianus.

January

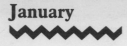

Rain in its grapeshot volleys; in the wood
disjointed elms crash, while the flying oaks
raucously thunder with a noise of surf.
Squalls sting and flurry in a rising smoke

that has cows huddle by an alder clump,
lashed, shifting mush, beaten by the whiplash
of a downpour that curds the flat to marsh,
and flogs the cowpath to a ruddled mash

of churn, footprints widening to lily-pads.
That red tractor, a Massey Ferguson
parked under a lean-to, is two-thirds mud;
rust's gobbled it from long inattention,

the farm is leaking outhouses, fallow,
red scraggy cockerels bickering in sheds
where winter pickers crated cauliflowers.
I blow my hands from blue to a chapped red

and squeeze uphill picking a middle path
between two pouring downstreams; here a fern
still lifts a pheasant's tail in a corner,
secret, enduring, like the crows that learn

to flaggingly batter into the rain,
embattled, barrel-rolling on the slide.
I get up to the wood's crown and shelter,
the fields dead-drop to meet a flooding tide,

the squall banging in with monotony,
relentless, inshore, not a gap-toothed wall
to break the head-on levelling of wind.
The wood cracks, it's as though an iron ball

draggingly thrashed the tree-tops, shaking out
sparklings of droplets. Now I start to break
for the nearest barn, coat a weighted sack,
my nose-dive startling a crow from its stake.

Foggy Days

A cabbage-head of fog occludes
distinction between land and sea,
my hands work like aircraft batons
clearing a space through which to see

my hands and then define my feet,
two blurs on an optician's card –
a myopic with glasses off,
each word breaking up into shards

that can't be pieced together. Boats
anchored offshore stand in a calm
not punctuated by seabirds,
but the monotonal alarm

of a foghorn's low, gravel-voiced
despair: a banshee wailing
for its mate across a salt marsh.
My fingertips find a railing,

a whitewashed wall, I'm flat against
the surface I had left, turned round
a compass needle that won't spin;
a damp chill works up off the ground,

each footstep sparkles with droplets.
The air I move silvers with fry,
flickering mercurial zigzags
across the grey pond of the sky,

there's no way in and no way out,
the sky's come down to anchor on
a coastline fogged out: a white sleep
pacifies the restless ocean.

Light's uniform, a monochrome
that's come to stay; I startle at
my backtread snapping a bracken.
Distance is a window-sill, flat

and levelled to a square fish-tank
I swim inside, scuffing up clouds
from the water's opacity,
a goldfish floating in a shroud.

The clamps are on; the roof won't lift,
I browse here a philatelist
too short-sighted for watermarks:
sharp gorse-spikes needle-prick my wrist.

Neutral

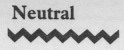

Green grass growing back through a stubble field
with chequered brushstrokes, thistle and chickweed
proliferating, you can feel the change –
the filtering of tiny air-borne seeds

drifting off microcosmically, the tap-
drip in the wood's the tick of poplar leaves
descending, yellow, skate-shaped, ribbed with green.
The air smells of woodsmoke, of hay-blond sheaves,

the magpie lifting's a blue and white fan
rapidly flurrying. I stare inside
a cavernous silo; a transistor
bubbles with its platitudinous tide

of universal misexpenditures,
the East and West, the claptrap of the day,
the tiny marks that don't make history,
the chaff that's either lost or blown away

through man's unregenerate militancy . . .
I cross a field and then another field,
the sky's a grey agate, the distant sea
is the blue-grey of a woodlouse's shield

locked tight into a ball in mute defence.
My footsteps terminate before the sea,
safe, neutral ground overrun by bracken,
the wild unclaimed kestrel's territory.

Distribution

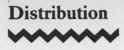

A cloud, and the dahlia's scarlet sun-core
darkens to crimson, parallels of light
striped on the turf between blue poplar trees
disappear like a bird's shadow in flight,

an empty turquoise deckchair faces out
across heathland, and where shadow translates
itself into a uniformity,
it equalizes; light thinning through slate-

blue cumulus effaces the hectic
Gauguin colours, orange and red poppies
that seem embers fanned from the explosive
dawn marigolds at Moorea, the sea

a reflective laval-red tiger-skin . . .
the blaze immobilized from dawn to dark.
Light breaks again in crescents through the trees
and finds the pink glow on the plane tree's bark,

the distribution's equal on this day,
high summer pewtering whatever's green,
touching each aspen leaf with a gold spot.
Days are like mushrooms, they grow up unseen,

ephemeral, they leave us with dust marks,
vaulting the fence in twos and threes not one,
the lizard signs the earth's crust with its tail,
the sitter tilts his chair back to the sun.

From where I stand an orange kite's afloat,
a triangular pennant played to stalk
the down-breeze, it's a fish-shape, a sting-ray,
it climbs up with the wind and starts to balk,

a mouse advancing by its nose through corn . . .
Shadow and light, they alternate all day,
a summer distributed through cloud-change
touches the magpie's blue and will not stay . . .

Momentum

The wind's an iron comb coiffing the grass,
you've notched your ear into that sibilance,
a shell's convoluted pressure of surf,
its whorls hum with the teeming distances,

blades threshed into a wiry running green –
a tornado to the cricket's alarm.
You pitch back in a rattan chair; plovers
dizzy to zebra-stripes over the barn,

their flight a moment forms a boomerang-
crescent, twenty arched into a whiplash.
Your rocking-chair is an ejector-seat,
I imagine you gone upon a flash,

a pin-dot figure projected through space,
hurtling forward like a pole-vaulter who
has gone up high into a freak air-stream,
a red tie snapping back against the blue,

the light the clear haze of a champagne glass . . .
Momentum gathers in this still-life frame,
the window is a screen transmitting how
gnats form a morris-dance over the grain

that stiffens in its partial ripening;
the scarecrow tinkers tin cans in the wind,
beating off magpies heckling as they rise.
Space floods us; placing an ear to the ground,

the pull grows stronger; you crouch forward now
straining for the horizon; a skylark's
a black butterfly at eight hundred feet,
its pointed wings lit by two orange sparks.

Shell Collection

The spiral whorl, the helix for an ear,
and each shell varnished to retain its sheen,
a serendipity's obsessive hoard,
here laid out in ivory, pink and green,

colours so richly diffused, yet subtle,
evolving from secreted pigment, might
be tintings of a water-colourist,
their coruscations arranged to highlight

each in its particular brilliance.
The thorny oysters have your pride of place,
their bramble-flower pinks and tangerines
have fragile spines, they're nebulae from space,

chrysanthemums, each spiky as a mace . . .
Close to the pelican's foot, the tritons
stripped of their encrustations would, if blown,
resemble the french-horn in its low tone,

or the deep sounding of a Baleen whale.
My eye seeks out each distinct mosaic,
the tiger cowrie, and the wall friezes
patterning cones, white hieroglyphs on black,

abstract pebblings, a desert-storm's dust haze.
I search for other rarities, the red
thumbprint-sized blotch upon the bleeding-tooth,
the cratered lunar map that's imprinted

on the volute, the double-bladed prong
on the venus comb murex, stood upright
it's a crossroads sign naming fifty towns.
I pass from shelf to shelf and focused light

accentuates what's beautiful in each.
The sea's two fields away, we hear it roar,
a thunderous flood-tide fuming between
the mixed pebbles of an Atlantic shore.

Summering

Months of desertion, and the cobwebs prink
floating trapezoids, suspension bridges
in every corner, gossamer gone slack
and slatted, threads unravelled from a ridge

that once were pegged out secure as guy-ropes . . .
I open windows and dispel the must
that's mulled in here all winter, a ferment
of rotting apples loads the air, and rust

has brightened on the sills, an ochre trail
that flakes at a finger. The plank jetty's
refurbished, paint has licked its warped struts white.
Three shades of blue, hydrangeas match a sea

that's vichy-clear, electric with mackerel.
I've come here looking for the same faces
who inhabited these sand-coves last year,
searching out the familiar places

to confirm their absence, a new beach set
has colonized the waterfront. I burn
to a chip of wood blackened by the fire,
my feet kick up cinders and when I turn

I see the cave-pitted coast disappear
in heat-haze, it's a blood-speck I follow,
and not the palpable firmness of turf,
a goat-path spiralling to a hollow

in which someone I've singled out sun-tans
upon a ledge. Or are they really there?
The map's deceptive, I have overshot
the place in its reality and stare

down at a glass pebble that seems to spin –
the afternoon's a white immobile glare,
the rock pool with its nervous cowering prawns
awaits the sea's return, its cooling air.

Hiving the Light

The sycamore leaf is a lizard's skin,
the light in falling ferments in the trees,
grape-yellow, beaten out like goldleaf, thin

as the striated gauze of a fly's wing.
You're stacking paintings, mostly sombre greens,
and where your head's in shadow a gold ring

surrounds it, making you the figurehead
embossed upon a newly minted coin.
Your black hair flickers a kingfisher thread.

A vintage, seasonal translucency
bottles our summer on the coast, the days
come clear, like mullet ruminatively

shoaled in glass shallows, browsing in suspense,
each fish distinct, but like leaves on a tree
responding to one current, stock-still, tense,

then gone as though the movement was one fish,
not twenty brittle with iridescence,
their scale-flash glinting with the startled swish

of a white horse's tail viewed through blue trees.
My focus sees things now in their own light,
each particle coloured by memory

is pollen of one flower known again
before its transformation in the hive.
We put the light to purpose, berries stain

the path, the holly's hectic fruiting glows.
I watch you move in and out of the light,
leaf shadows dart like fish across the windows.

192

Migration

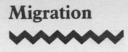

Now is the time of migration, a mist
confirms a seasonal stillness to the air;
birds spar and dart, unable to resist

the quickening assertion of that pole
which twice yearly channels them through air-flues
over continents that might be atolls

their homing stimuli's so accurate.
The air's electric with their shrill furore;
a swallow's zigzag to a spiral gate,

to strum back to the trilling of a wire
vibrant with birds, denotes the urgency
each has acquired, crisp as the crackling fire

a bee emblazons. The season's turned gold,
the russet plumage of the equinox
is speckled chartreuse and toad-brown, a cold

drops early. Bird after bird in pre-flight
expectation's nervously triggered to go,
migrants who'll fly unveeringly by night

as well as day, caught in the powerful sweep
a lighthouse throws, or seen as silhouettes
against the lunar disc. I fish the deep

channels inshore, and apprehensively.
Conger and dogfish might begin to bark
from the oil-black. The bay's a flat ivy-

leaf darkening from an ink-tinctured sea.
Everything groups before the air flickers
with an increased, audible vibrancy,

and then they're gone, the swallows first, gone high,
their bodies kindled by such energy
their blue shapes dive like arrows through the sky.

September Cycle

So looking down all summer from the cape
at you sunbathing in metallic gold
or frost-silver, I came to know your shape
sunning on a lilo, or hunched in folds

of a beach cloak, a book upon your knee,
the light etherealizing you; the bay
a flinty blue bowl siphoned from a sea
turned moody on the change. Looking away,

your eyes perspicuously shaded by
blue glasses, sometimes I would catch your stare
and deflect it, pointing up at the sky
where like a coil unleashed the drum of air

was swallows beating seaward – energy
so volatile it passed through one like light,
and wrenched one's head to face that migratory
feathered arrow in its shrill shaft of flight.

I came to know you the way memory
selects an image as a cameo,
your profile set in turquoise, lucidly
strained against a night sky of indigo,

or lonely, standing on a small jetty,
a figure also anxious to migrate
with gusting birds. Each day, predictably,
I'd find you waiting to anticipate

the sun's breaking through at noon for an hour's
concentrated and wasp-gold heat, a tall
golfing umbrella beside you for showers
that rinsed the cape silver. The plaintive call

of oystercatchers emphasized how still
the bay had grown. I left you on the beach,
our unbroken silence growing too shrill,
your body ripe for autumn like a peach.

Late Year Fog

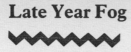

They're stacked above the tideline, lobster pots
wintering in the cove. The fishermen
have beached their dinghies, flipped them upside down
for rain to pummel. Now mist drops again,

obscuring the backdrop to a dead year,
its dissolute links eroded, its spark
a coal patinated in grainy ash.
The wires are down, a taxi hunts the dark,

laying out traces for a small hotel
couched in its cat's-cradle of country lanes –
the white hart on its sign jumps with the wind,
and with a clatter rights itself again.

Turned soil, high hedges, and diffused droplets
of mist silvering, now a tractor's sway
weaves lurchingly out to menace traffic,
its tailboard unlit, it at last gives way

caterpillaring down a hairfine track
to a loaf-shaped farm and its fuzz of thatch.
The dark's a thistlehead, in a call-box
cold hands flick for a number with a match,

but can't get through. The year's dying in thin
voices cabled beneath the sea, a man
coddled by bourbon speaks to someone here
from a snowed-in loft high in Manhattan,

snow-ploughs shunting the drifts to yellow waste.
The taxi's found its scent, its red brake-lights
work hard on the spiral descent to where
a country inn is half absorbed by night

and half lit up, it bears a holly wreath
interleaved with ivy and mistletoe.
Someone slams a log and its embers flush
from a blue wood-ash to an orange glow.

Painting Water

Its scent already there before
we dropped down out of an oak wood,
feet planing the slippery incline,
trailing, until breathless we stood

in a brambled divide between
two gradients alike as steep
and treed by palsied creaking elms.
For months the stream had been asleep,

we'd painted its lethargic crawl,
its drugged, passive diminuendo,
keeping a low head over stones,
it seemed to be hauling its flow

out of a deadweight in the hills,
and arrived thin, a stranded eel,
its gills pumping for oxygen.
Its nerves seemed no longer to feel

for the obstructions in its path,
it sickened khaki with the drought,
a trickle puddling to an ooze.
Now after rains it drives its rout

of sticks upon its bull-broad back,
it is a logrolling packhorse
at full gallop, frothing to brake
over stones then resume its course,

the sinews taut as violin strings,
the eddies chiffon ruching where
the current's tendrils circulate.
No longer shrinking from our stare,

it wears a snake's markings of leaves,
the torrent lashing it won't let
up now, it smashes chestnut pods
into the ferment, branches fret,

the deadwood lopped by the big gale.
Waterproofed we assimilate
each water-stroke as a brushstroke,
a thin wrist dealing out a spate,

insuperable, rushing towards
an outlet where it will grow tame,
its force siphoned off by the sea,
an angry bride losing her name.

After Montale
[1985]

Rifts

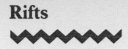

in memory of Eugenio Montale
The ivy leaf's a diamond-lit frog's back
after the sudden impingement of rain,
and drops ricochet from the waxing black

of the sloe-berry, and the queen of hearts
is multiplied on each fallen pear leaf.
If a bird drops down it's quick to depart,

its eye flashing faster than a raindrop,
and coloured with the premonitory South.
The woodlouse locks fast in the log's slow rot.

Alive, you followed rifts, a kingfisher's
brilliant flare igniting the slow pool,
then imperceptibly lost in azure,

or the smoke spiral of a ship's funnel
hanging in a slow S while mist dispersed
to a rainbow. On cobbled flats runnels

tingled with light – each sea-pool a mirror
pointing you to the still more vibrant stars,
and sitting late the porcupine's tremor

was the first hint of storm, as a fish net
lifted by the gust concurred with lightning.
All life's the startled bolt of a mullet

disturbed by a shadow and gone so quick
we think it forever in migration.
You watched for breaks and knew the erratic

wavering of the sea-bound butterfly
touched on the very pulse of light, and drew
from its frenetic course a harmony

all light-borne creatures have. Word after word
catches fire in your work as mist singes,
and through its red hoop darts the migrant bird.

Arsenio

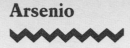

The wind picks up dust in frantic eddies,
grit sprays the rooftops and smokes across squares
where horses sniff the ground, fidgetingly
tied up before the decanter glitter
of hotel windows.
You take the promenade facing the sea
on this afternoon of frenetic squalls,
the sky, the storm-palette of a rainbow,
is answered by a beak-rattle of castanets.

That sign has you follow a new orbit.
The horizon's a lead whirlpool of spray
haystacked above the frenzy of the bay;
a seething, tornadoing black cloudhead
drives in; the boiling spume dazzles.
Your foot slides on the shingle, weed ensnares
each scuttled step. The blindingly delirious
moment's the one you've anticipated,
it is a link in an unmoving chain . . .

Through the goose-hissing of palms, a sudden
urgency of violins competes
with the thunder's detonation, the crash
of metal plates welded upon a floor . . .
In intermittent lulls the white dog star
floods a blue reach, before the scissor flash
of lightning branches into a forked tree
of indigo. A gypsy kettledrum
peters out on that note.

You go down into a blazing darkness
that turns the sultry noon into midnight;
globes of light rock on the moored fishing fleet,
the sky and sea are indivisibly
blueblack, except where a trawler's stern light
winks through; acetylene drifts on the air.

203

The squall subsides in slow trembling raindrops
pocking the steaming earth. A liquid sheet
glazes the town; the pummelled tents cave in,
the soggy paper lanterns hit the street.

Stranded among sodden wickers, straw mats,
you are a reed dragging its clammy roots
out of the river bed, hysterical
with crackling electricity you reach
towards an empty interposing void
that spins, and flings you back against the wall
on which a frozen mirror holds
you transfixed to the star-shine of dead things.

If a word reaches you, or a gesture
arrests your flux Arsenio,
it's a sign of temporal appeasement,
a gap in the closed circuit of a future
you would have throttled. In a reddening glow
a wind lights up the ashes of the stars.

Summer

The kestrel's filtered shadow leaves no trace
on dry bushes, but tricks a darkened cross
on the heath's green awakening with spring.
The earth reflects the blue mirror of space.

Now that the year returns, perhaps you too
Arethusa show in the twisted gleam
of a trout shouldering upstream,
dear child whom death plucked from your fragile web.

Things catch light in a blaze. A shoulderblade
burns like a nugget exposed to the sun;
the cabbage butterfly flickers, a thread
suspends the spider over boiling surf –

and something imperceptible quivers,
and won't pass through the needle's eye, but burns . . .

Too many lives are needed to make one.

The Eel

~~~~~~~~

The eel, that cold-water siren
migrating from the Baltic
to our warm Mediterranean,
is streamlined to resist the flood
in foment, and keeps low, its quick
malleable pokerhead, snaking
from hairline to hairline crevice,
working upstream, so sinuous
it might pass through a wedding ring,
at last reaches the coppered light
filtering through green chestnut trees
and lies there, fired to a tabby
cat's orange markings in water
slowed from rivulets that streak across
the Apennines to the Romagna;
and contorted to a whiplash
catches fire like a pitch-arrow
in the arid craters left by
drought where mosquitoes simmer,
suddenly adopts the storm glow
of a spark that points to how
embers quicken in their extinction
round the stump of a dead tree-bole,
and how the brief, iridescent
blazing of its tornado flash,
is twin to the one between your eyes,
mad sister finding like a moth
ecstasy in the flame's surprise.

New Stanzas

Decisively you extinguish the last
red tobacco shreds in the crystal dish –
an heirloom left over from your rich past,
much as the retinue of your chessboard,
ivory knights and bishops will outlast
the sinuous smoke spirals you dispel
ceilingwards, a mist that obscures the hoard
of knuckled gold that burns on your fingers.

The heaven-sent messenger who disclosed
ethereal cities of the rainbow
to you in reverie has disappeared.
Your eyes snap back from that unseen window
to agitations of smoke, and a pack
of troubled thoughts bred by the underworld
clouds the features of each heraldic face.
You wear fear like a mule a heavy pack.

Watching you thus, I doubt whether you know
what game is played beneath you on the square.
Chain-smoking, you set up a beacon's glow
against the marauding black wolf of death.
Your vigil shows this, and it's in your stare,
a lightning awareness of other fires
staked out around you in the pit below.
You sniff their embers and await the flare.

The Customs House

You don't recall the Customs House, that lair
perched like a crow's-nest, so precariously
above the sheer rock-fall to the breakers,
that hung there as a desolate shelter
for the mad torrent of your thoughts to hive
in, restless, unrequited.

For years the sirocco's whipped paint to shale,
and the sound of your laughter is a gale
that spins the maddened compass needle aimlessly
as the wrong throw of dice your words turn up.
You won't recall, a sea-blur hangs over
your memory, a thread unwinds.

I hold an end of it, but the rocked house
recedes; the sea-warped weathervane clatters,
and wind ferociously snaps at pennants.
I keep my thread, fishing for you who cower
alone there, breathless in the spinning dark.

On the shifting horizon the red light
of a tanker flickers upon the edge . . .
Is this the crossing of our threads where surf
seethes in its boiling-pot beneath the cliff?
You don't remember our jagged outpost,
or which of us remains, and which goes lost.

At Fiesole

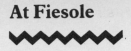

Insistently a cricket penetrates
the green leaf coating of the vegetable.
A scent of camphor permcates,
but can't deter the moths from entering
books in which they'll stiffen to a bookmark.
A treecreeper investigates the bole
of an elm, then runs up into a branch
of the sun-arrested green foliage –
another liveflash, a transient gleam,
the scarlet ivy flicks its trail of sparks.

Sirocco

The sirocco's a flame-thrower
seething over the arid soil
in dust-trails. Look up there –
the sky's glintingly luminous,
a single cloud's chased like a hare.
Hours of confusion, things shiver,
or run like water through fingers
that can't hold on. Everything's
tested to the extreme, is proved,
disproved, made visible, or else
wavers in the hissing tumult
without a moment's let-up.
I too am whirled adrift,
and rattled like an agave
in a rock fissure, resist the spin,
as seaweed undulatingly regroups
after the sea's battering, jarred assault,
it pincer motions in that rush.
My brain throbs to explode, its balance
gone, a kite without a string,
I feel my rootlessness, my transfixed stare,
whipped by the scorched brutality of air.

The Sunflower

Bring me the sunflower and I'll transplant
it in my garden's burnt salinity.
All day its heliocentric gold face
will turn towards the blue of sky and sea.

Things out of darkness incline to the light,
colours flow into music and ascend,
and in that act consume themselves, to burn
is both a revelation and an end.

Bring me that flower whose one aspiration
is to salute the blond shimmering height
where all matter's transformed into essence,
its radial clockface feeding on the light.

The Black Trout

At evening bent over sidling water,
graduates in economics,
doctors of divinity,
are intense in their scrutiny.
The trout senses their reflections and flares,
showing a coral black rainbow
like one of your curls come undone
in the bath, you are shadowy
in the depths of your office block.

Point of the Mesco

At dawn, unbending flights of partridges
skimmed over the quarry's skyline,
the smoke from explosives lazily puffed
in eddies up the blind rockface. The ridge
brightened. The trail of foam left by the pilot boat's
beaked prow settled into illusory
white flowers on the surface of the sea.

I still recall the path down here I tracked
once like a troubled dog. The swell pitches
between rocks and the backwash cargoes straw.
Nothing's changed, the wet gravel's still shaken
by detonations, the hunched stonebreakers
bend and huddle from the wind.

The bleak landscape brings back something of you.
A pneumatic drill gouges into rock
and smashes granite. A smoke flare goes up:
I smart, and redefine with clarity
your rare features, now they return to me,
jerky, imprecise, for a moment there,
then blasted by the next charge into air.

The Shadow of the Magnolia

The Japanese magnolia's shadow thins
to less density now the purple buds
have fallen. A cicada's drumming note
sounds from the top. The season's unison
of voices is checked; the raging godhead
no longer ploughs through, killing for rebirth,
granting his victims leave to suck their blood.
It was easier to burn out, to die
at the first flurry of wings, at the first
encounter with the enemy, short-circuit
and go. Now a harder trial begins,
but not for you, fieldfare, scorched by the sun,
and now flitting above the cold wharf-piles
of the river, in whom, zenith, nadir
cancer and capricorn failed to register.
The war of elements was enacted within
the pad of your fragile skull brushed silver
by the frost. Now nature's reserves retreat . . .
The cutting edge of the engraving file
falls silent, the empty husk of the singer's voice
is a sugared glass-powder underfoot,
the magnolia's shadow turns lividly
upon itself. It's autumn, it's winter,
it's the beyond in reaches of the sky
I throw myself into, the spiral jump
of a mullet breaking water to die
beneath a new moon, that leap means

                    Goodbye.

Hitlerian Spring

A white cloud of moths crazily halo
the globes of streetlamps, their spotting shadows
could have one believe that one's foot crackles
on sparkling sugar. Summer's here? the chill
of its first month extends from the orchards
to the sandpits at Maiano.

A motorcyclist in black leather roars
through the high street; his supporters salute
and unravel their swastikas.
The small town's shop windows are boarded up,
even the butcher's whose wreaths of holly
decorated the heads of slaughtered goats.
Blood stains the hands of pacifists, a wild
exchange of wings leads to a beak ripped throat.
The water goes on eating at the shore,
moths singe and frazzle on the harbour lamps.

Was it for nothing that roman candles
lit the horizon of San Giovanni,
and valedictions promising pledges
reverted to hostility?
But there was hope in the bud that distilled
its clemency over ice-bound rivers,
and in the messengers of Tobias
seeding the future with gold stars.
Warfare shrivelled the fragrant heliotrope,
a fire that hissed like pollen angrily
fuelled to the cutting edge of a blizzard.

Spring's still a festival if it freezes
the open scar of war, a murderous
red ice. In you, immutable Clizia,
I look for the ever returning sun,
its blinding dazzle a sunflower's eye . . .

Perhaps the sirens and discord of bells
that howl against the bombers' night attack
will fall silent one dawn, and a blue sky
dispel the aerial terror, and white wings
flash over arid wadis of the south . . .

Correspondences

A vaporous mirage, the horizon
comes nearer announcing the shrill yatter
of a green woodpecker.

Discoveries are for the outstretched hand
searching the underwood for a gold web
stringing up in its littered points,
a toxic fruit that ripens to nightmare.
In the pond's mirror you can see the car
of Bacchus break through, in its wake, the yelp
of rams stampeding from the dust-bowl hills,
whinny to blood-heat on the air . . .

She won't return, the girl who drove that flock,
and yet I recognize her in the dust
kicked up by pelting hooves, and in the flight
of birds going. The plain's a flogged drum-skin.
On glinting roofs I catch the flash of light
mirrored by a passing express, hell-bent
to meet the steaming coast, its funnel blares.

Delta

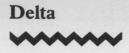

How often, bound to you, my secrecy hurt
like fishing twine pulled tight over a wrist.
I made you nervous by being alert

to each nuance of our web-like moods.
You, who would break like a fish from the flood
trailing intimate knowledge of the void,
as now with the expenditure of rain,
green brightens, battening to the sumac's stain.

Everything about you's enigmatic.
Sometimes you seem a wraith strayed from the pit,
or a figure pronounced in silhouette
against the coast path. Surf in sudden fits
smokes round the headland, or subsides in calm.

I can't define nor make you palpable.
You're out there in the lightning flash that plays
over the haze, as now a hooting tug
comes with its stern lights flashing through the bay.

On a Letter Unwritten

For the recurrent blueness of sea dawns,
or for an instinctive thread that they chase
into hours and years, today the dolphins
in pairs disport with their young in the bay.
Your homing's different; it finds me out
with the swiftness of lightning searing space.
I cannot face you nor yet run away;

the earth's a tiny cone and shelterless.
And still it holds back, the scarlet furnace
of evening reddening above the sea.
Prayer becomes torture, and distraction's worse,
searching for a bottle below the sheer
rockface, fishing for a message. The wave
emptily breaks on rocks at Finisterre.

Eclogue

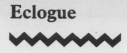

It was a ritual: we would lose ourselves
in the silver-blue of my olive trees,
the orchard loud with bird-song, slow runnels,
our feet scuffing the silver blades of leaves.
Disjointed thoughts found a coherency
in the propitiatory calm.

Now the cerulean marbling's stormed by clouds.
The garden pine telescopes into space,
and through the grey a luminous porthole
of light develops in intensity.
Your elbow breaks a radial spider's web
as part of your new inconsistency.
Somewhere a train clatters, picking up speed,
a shot shivers the sky, rattling pigeons
nosedive in compass-spinning formation,
and with the rising wind you seem to burn
within the rind of a bitter past life.
Explosive barking rages from the hills.

Our summer interlude protracts itself
in the smouldering light that magnifies
a point of exit on the horizon.
The bean plant's strafed to a stringy tangle.
Nothing seems opportune, no rapid flight,
no sudden outburst of temerity.
Only the cicadas outlast this squall
in their shrill clamour of importunacy.
Listening to the wind it's you I recall,
a bacchante, ivy-wreathed, streaming with blood . . .

Now as the sickle moon lifts a white horn,
I remember our inconclusive nights.
The finger that you scratched on the world's face
is a dust-mark the sirocco's erased.

220

Disturbed once, we walked where the thistles shorn
of flowers were white blowballs in the dark.
In my country this hour anticipates
the hare's lightning-bolt, its whistle of fright.

Under the Rain

A cloud-dash, and your house obscured by haze
is fogged out like a point in memory
that's ceased to flicker. The palm beads with rain.
The cat's-cradle of my mind slips a knot,
its galvanized hothouse eats through my nerves . . .

Por amor de la fiebre . . . your figure swirls
and joins me in the dance. An awning flares
redly, a window casement's shut.
Somewhere above me in the mountain air
the egg-shell slope is slushed into a slide,
life flutters between light and shade.

Your record crackled across the courtyard –
*Adios Muchachos, compañeros
de mi vida*. I still hold to the words,
seeking the one gap in the milling round
of possibilities, the break or leap
into the unknown by which you are found.

I follow the luminous breaks in cloud,
smoke from a ship spirals from the skyline,
a bright rift clears . . .
                      In you I realize
the daring of the stork's migratory shape,
lifting off from the misty pinnacle,
head pointing like an arrow for the Cape.

Beach in Versilia

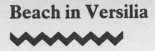

I pray to the dead that they pray for me,
alive we ask fulfilment of the inexplicable.
I look to the horizon where a wash
of sky and sea
touches the windows in the evening rays.
It's seldom now a goshawk planes the blue,
or a flying white cutter sweeps the bay.
I think back, was it yesterday

beds of artfully coloured zinnia
watered by poker-stiff starched grandmothers
gave on to lichened courtyards where a cat
snoozed in the lining of a gardener's hat,
or smokily gambolled across the lawn? . . .
The landscape's changed. The skyline's restoreyed.
Houses look out across descending dunes
and beach umbrellas to a scorching sand
that once nurtured trees dear to my childhood –
the wild pine, fig, the eucalyptus tree.

Memories crowd back of those childhood days,
their resonance, their peopled solitude,
cicadas chirring through the siesta
haziness of my drowning sleep,
at night the buzzing of mosquitoes
syphoning blood from my skin.
Or waking at night in the corner room,
I'd watch shadows pummel the catch of eels,
forcing the bones back to stiffen the tail
before excising them. Later that day
I'd hear the swish of garden rakes and shears
endlessly competing with accretions
of weed in the green nursery –
evergreens forming a windbreak from the sea.

Years of inshore reefs, sea horizons,
a child's recognition of the humanly
purposeful, acts named by continuity
of generations – I would gasp
for the underwater breathing of the priest fish,
swallow fish, the wolfishly marauding lobster
with its nutcracker pincers . . .
the buoyant flight of mice from palm to palm.
Time then was measurable. Now it lifts me
with a sirocco's tempestuous motion.

Times at Bellosguardo

The horizon arches towards the hills,
the beehive murmur of evening dies there,
and trees converse with the ticking of sand
grained by the wind. How crystalline the air,
the symmetry of columns, thatched willows,
and in the gardens you might see stone wolves
caught in midflight above a pond
beaded by a fountain's glow . . .
There life's more tranquil, there's a fluency
in the sapphire light that arrests the hills.
What's meaningful there
shows up in flashes – steam rising from a bend,
voices at evening from terraced gardens,
laughter from rooftops or a patio,
the flickering of interleaved branches
through which one sees the luminous heavens.
Words aim their flight there – a straining arrow . . .

Desolate on the slope,
the magnolia's leaves turn
a greenish-brown. The wind
tests icy groundfloor rooms,
and if a concordance
of distorted voices return
upon the air they're lost
in the bush's twinkling flurry,
each leaf lit by the wind.
But we who live are lost
in the prism of the minute,
our frantic desire to escape
the net, ends in delirium,
sweat, and the consciousness of acts
mirrored to infinity,
a pendulum's fugitive count
between what passes and what stays,

225

faceted by sun or rain.
Up here there's no way out,
we die knowingly, or we choose
a conscious transience
that also leads to death.

History is lost between the galleries
and pillared statuary. Whatever lives
on here is in the pigment of the stone
that gave itself to images,
honour, love, the dice of the stars,
unwavering conviction.
Persistence is in the spirit of a place,
the void sounded, the boundaries measured,
and in the invisible signature
of that spirit which simply is
in its unrepeatable containment.
Perhaps it enters the closed sanctuary
and finds the serial to the mystery
with the fine point of a picklock.

Syria

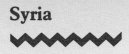

The ancients said that poetry
is the dream-ladder to God. My work
lacked that directive, but I knew it the day
your voice spoke through me
restoring my own, up there in a flock
of summit-clouds and goats
bursting out of a ditch to crop blackthorn
and wire-grass, and the opposing faces
of sun and moon fused in one mirror,
the car had broken down and an arrow
of blood on a boulder pointed
the way to Aleppo.

Angularity

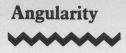

I should have had the angularity,
the pocked moon-face of pebbles eroded
by the sea's mouth, bitten and then spat free,
a fragment outside time, a salt-rimed chip
of the untiring universal will.
Instead, I am a contemplative man,
my eye focused on the transient bubbling
of life's inner source; a man who defers action
for the indestructible lens of vision.
I wanted to eradicate the globular
termite's persistent drilling, the lever's
hairline imprecision in locking the gears
of the universal spin, and I saw
the microscopic dissection of time
in the molecular dance of atoms.
What I needed was a knife that cuts clean,
a mind triggering the freedom to choose
the uncharred text from its flame-brittle page.
I regret nothing; again you unknot
my inner fishline tangle with your talk.
Now your delirium climbs starward in its rage.

Indian Serenade

Our moment comes when the evening reddens,
a long eyebrow that arches from the sea,
flooding the park, tinting the aloes pink.

If you can make believe you're here with me,
then I can follow you invisibly,
aware that abjuration of your power
takes me step by step to the edge . . .

If your life held me back on a thin ledge
then I could lend you an anatomy,
a face, perfection of a shape.

But it's not true. The polyp that insinuates
its octopus tentacles between rocks
could syphon life from you. You feed him blood

and he grows inky blue.
You're part of him and yet you think you're you.

Wind and Flags

The wind carries a scent of spray
that beads the scorched inland valleys,
it blows your hair into the sparks
an incandescent log spits free,

and pins your dress tightly across
a figure sharpened in outline.
Sculptured by the wind on these heights,
you look down, how the boulders shine

like nuggets on the valley floor.
The breeze that cradled your hammock
all summer, rocking you in flight,
now cuts through with a numbing shock . . .

Time never refashions a day,
the wheat ear splits, already we
are figures in a brief fable,
a nerve charred black by history.

From here we see them, a handful
of huts crouched into the rockface,
banners and pennants stream from them,
a flag picks up the pull of space.

Bewilderment spins us around,
a terrifying sense that there
in the portent of evening wait
the scarlet and black messengers . . .

Costa San Giorgio

A light in zigzags menaces the road
and dusts it copper, as the lamplighter
coasts downhill like a coot breasting water,
a steel ladder saddled on his shoulder.
Light answers light around the square,
shadows deploy then settle in corners.

The circle of lights, a constricting hoop,
shows no break in its circuit. The moon's ash.
Only at the far end of a tunnel
is there a light less fixed in its severity,
a phosphorescent frost of night insects
that crackle in their brittle shells.

And picked out by the lights a bronze statue
shows a tarnished patina of green rime.
Scorched by the heat, inanimately dull,
its gesture entertains no miracles,
it wears time like a punished bell,
grave, unpolished as a campaign medal.

Everything's rigid here; the only dance
is in the magic circle of the lights.
Maritornes no longer unhooks the lamp
from the stable-architrave. It is night,
and no guide offers us a safe passage . . .

What startles is the screeching of the years
on rusty hinges, a plaintive grating
that opens to a treacherous descent,
and at the bottom of the weedy stairs
comes the mute watchman's tightening of the screw . . .
If a clock chimes behind a bolted door
it carries with it the half muffled thud
of a child's puppet falling from its chair.

Xenia I (1964–6)

1

Little fly-like insect mosca
here beside me in the blue-dark,
you appeared while I was reading
Deutero-Isaiah,
but your myopic vision
was blurred as my telescoping
to find you in light grained like bark.

2

Without wings or antennae
your orbit was foreshortened,
the bible losing its pages,
thumbed, riffled, exfoliated,
lightning rinsing an ink-black sky,
the storm imminent but withheld.
If you were its conductor,
you blazed a trail leaving me
with nerve-jabs of telepathy . . .

3

A single room in the Saint James in Paris,
so too in the mock Byzantine goldleaf
of your old hotel in Venice.
Alone now, I search the telephone booth's
intimate but alienating closet,
and whirr the finger-tarnished dial,
tensing for your expectant voice.
At such moments death's only a half truth.

4

In secrecy we'd devised a whistle,
a mutual signal of recognition
for the next world. I'm practising it now
hoping we're already dead and don't know it.

5
I'll never know now if you thought of me
as your faithful distempered dog
heeling invisibly. To others
you were a pink-eyed myopic insect
ensnared in the champagne popping ennui
of high society. Those mannequins
never perceived the perspicuity
with which you unmasked their *trompe-l'oeil* hubris
with your bat's radar humming in the dark.

6
You left no line of prose or poetry,
no improvisation. That was your charm,
and correspondingly my irritant.
Snagged on a rusty barb of self-loathing,
my fear was that you'd throw me back into
the croaking swampool of neoterics.

7
I blow our whistle but you don't appear.
In Azucena in the second act
the agonized pain of this dust-stormed world
is for those rooted here
who imagine the other world's elsewhere.

8
Your words, impulsive, equivocatory,
remain within my audial memory,
only the accent's changed, the colour too.
Now I must learn how to decipher you
in the electric tick of the telex,
and in the blue spiralling smoke-rings
of my Brissago cigars.

9
Listening was your only way of seeing.
The telephone bill has diminished now.

10
If she prayed it was to Saint Anthony
to rescue umbrellas left on the train,
the ephemera of Hermes' cloakroom,
sometimes for those before us, sometimes me.
Prayer's how many minims of our death solution? . . .

11
Hysterical at times, I shared your storms,
the aftermath was unconstrained laughter.
These moods anticipated the screening
of your private Last Judgement, never shown,
only mirrors have access to our private lives.

12
Spring with its pinks arrives at a mole's pace.
They're still with me your obsessive topics –
the adverse effects of antibiotics,
the steel-pin riveted in your thigh-bone,
the operational aberrancies . . .

Spring's here again with its gull's feather mists,
long days that open doors into the sun . . .
Now I'll no longer hear your diver's breath
fighting the remorseless backwash of time.
If death's a logistic problem, your ghost's
an air coloured balloon's weight above the lime.

13
Your brother died young, a leaf caught in flame.
You were the dishevelled child affecting

a cool composure looking out at me
from your oval portrait. He wrote music,
unheard, unpublished, if it still remains
it's yellowed in a lumber trunk, or been
unconsciously assimilated by someone
and reinterpreted. It's odd that he
who never knew me should be accorded
a quirky posthumous fame by the memories
I have from you. Love grows stronger with death.
Living, we're shadows blown out by a breath.

14
They designate my poetry
as one of unbelonging, but its yours,
you who've thinned out of form into the light.
They say that poetry synthesizes
animation, but still deny that law
by which the tortoise is swift as the thunderbolt.
You alone knew that motion is stasis,
the void a plenum of stars, the clear sky
the most diffuse of clouds.
By this I understand your long voyage
imprisoned in bandages and casts,
yet there's compensation in the thought
that one or together we're still alone.

Xenia II

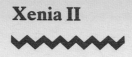

I
Death didn't concern you.
Your dogs had died, so too the doctor
for the insane we nicknamed mad uncle,
and your mother with her frog risotto –
a Milanese idiosyncrasy,
and your father who now sits watching me
from his miniature, closed to what he sees.
You wanted no part in that mystery.

It was I who'd attend funerals,
cowed in a taxi, skirting the edges
of grief, viewing from the periphery.
Even life registered little with you –
its obsessive viri, vanity, greed,
and that universal concupiscence
which turns men into wolves.

A *tabula rasa*: except
for a point beyond my comprehension
which you called your own.

2
You'd often recall (I less) Mr Cap.
'Twice I met him on the bus at Ischia,
a lawyer from Klagenfurt, look his greeting card
says he would like to visit us.'

He came. I had to tell him everything.
Speechless, his mouth frozen in a rictus,
he gagged on silence then rose poker-stiff,
bowed and assured me he'd send his regards . . .

Only implausible people came to know you,
dear Dr Cap, demented Celia,
but what became of her?

236

3
It went missing, our rusty tin shoehorn,
our inveterate talisman brandished
even among pinchbeck and stucco statuettes.
Was it at the Danieli that I forgot
to give it asylum in my suitcase,
or was it Hedia our chambermaid
flicked it into the Canalazzo? . . .
How could I have written asking the return
of an inconsequential strip of tin,
and yet our lives balanced on that small thing
Hedia had saved as though it was a ring.

4
Emerging with temerity
from the furnace-throat of Mongibello
or the swordfish-jaw of ice-straits
your uncommon ability
to unmask was pronounced.

Our doctor Mangano
was similar. Exposed as the whiphand
of the Black Shirt terrorists,
he smiled, contemplating his wrist.

You too on the edge of a precipice
combined terror and rightness in one music.

5
Your arm in mine, I've descended so many stairs,
and now your weightless absence unsettles
my steps. Our voyage was a brief matchflame . . .
Mine continues, only I've relinquished
bookings, time-tables, our itinerary,

237

but mostly I've dispensed with those who think
reality's a rationalization.

A lifetime facing steps, your frailty . . .
We were an odd insect beaming four eyes,
and yours although myopic were the true,
and focused where most cannot see.

6
The wine-seller watched the fire in the wine –
Inferno. You shrunk enquiringly and said,
it's enough to have felt the blaze for a lifetime . . .

7
'I've never felt I belonged to this earth.'
'If that's so,' you replied, 'my grip's frailer?'

'You've savoured life in homeopathic
doses. But as for me I don't exist . . .'

8
'And Paradiso? Is there a paradise?'
'I think so, but sauternes are out of fashion.'

9
They always frightened you, black processions,
nuns, widows, unceremonious mourners,
You thought that even the great seeing eye
shut tight in an eclipse at sight
of their contrast with the light.
                              Your discretion
had you refer to god in lower case.

10
That interminable search, then I found you
in a bar in the Avenida

da Libertade; you had no Portuguese
except for a single word, Madeira.
Your wineglass was embellished with a shrimp.

That evening my work found comparison
with Carducci and those illustrious
Portuguese with unpronounceable names.
I watched you in your bar corner,
amused, diffident at my sudden fame.

11
Resurfacing into the field of time,
Celia telephoned. You are well, I say,
your presence seems more real, more composite,
and she, 'I take it that she's somewhere else' . . .
How can I explain you are anyway.
From the end of the wire a mosquito
buzz tells me you've hung up. I speak to the air.

12
Hawks, up high, telescoping,
always outside of the range of your sight.
But there were others, one at Etretat,
eyeing the flustered nosedives of its young,
and two above the Delphic Way,
as yet, no concentration in their flight,
a scuffle of soft feathers, harmless beaks.

You liked life torn to shreds,
the circuit smashed, holes in the web,
escape from the inexorable net.

13
Your father as a child – the daguerrotype's
a moth-beige nineteenth-century sepia.

It's there as a reminder of my lack
of pedigree.
I try to scan yours like a tree-climbing ivy,
but we're not horses, we lack a stud book,
and those who claim a part in the tracery
are as nonexistent as we to them.
But something gave a continuity –
the pool rises from the capricious shower.

14
The rising flood's floated the furniture,
paintings, coloured maps, papers double-locked
in an underworld cellar, all afloat.
Perhaps they staged their own naumachia,
the red Moroccan volumes and Du Bos'
interminable dedications, the red wax stamp
of Ezra's beard, Alain's Valéry,
the original of the Canti Orfici,
hairless shaving brushes, ephemera,
and all your brother Silvio's music.
Filmed over by gasoline for two weeks,
they fought the loss of their identity.
I, too, can scarcely break the waterline,
my civil status always dubious.
It's not the flood that's dislodged me, rather
a lifetime's disbelief in reality.
My courage in facing it was your own.
Even if you knew it you couldn't see.